'My Darling Danny'
Letters from Mary O'Connell
to her Son Daniel, 1830–1832

Edited by

Erin I. Bishop

CORK UNIVERSITY PRESS

For Mary

First published in 1998 by
Cork University Press
Cork
Ireland

British Library Cataloguing in Publication Data

A CIP catalogue record for this book is available from the British Library.

ISBN 1 85918 173 2

Typesetting by Red Barn Publishing, Skeagh, Skibbereen

Printed in Ireland by ColourBooks, Baldoyle, Co. Dublin

M 104, 911 | 920 O'CON
£8. 95

Contents

Acknowledgements

I would like to thank the staff at the National Library of Ireland for all their assistance, for granting me access to this collection, and for allowing these letters to be transcribed in full. I would also like to thank the Office of Public Works for the use of the portrait on the cover. In addition, I owe a substantial debt to my former colleagues at the Lincoln Legal Papers Project, in Springfield, Illinois, USA, who taught me all I know about documentary editing. Finally, I would like to thank my editor, David Fitzpatrick, for his advice and guidance, as well as his patience.

Introduction

Simple, unassuming letters between a mother and her son are a rarity in the records of the past, and until quite recently such private documents were thought to be of little significance. As a result, many such collections were discarded for their lack of 'relevant' subject-matter. Mary O'Connell's correspondence with her young son Danny, for example, has been preserved, not for its insights into nineteenth-century Irish society and culture, but for the sole reason that she was the wife of Daniel O'Connell, the 'Liberator'.

Raised at Derrynane in County Kerry and educated on the continent, O'Connell was called to the Irish bar in 1798. The rising of that year provoked O'Connell to take a stance against violence as a means to political change. Drawn to political action, he took up the cause of Catholic Emancipation. He became the leader of the radical Catholic Committee and later, in 1823, founded the Catholic Association with the goal of securing Emancipation through constitutional means. Riding the Munster Circuit, he built up an enormous legal practice and quickly became known as a tireless worker and skilful defender. His legal practice and courtroom performances became the platform on which he built growing political support among the masses as 'Counsellor' O'Connell. In 1828 O'Connell was returned for County Clare in the celebrated by-election. While Mary O'Connell's son was suffering the tedium of boarding-school life, her husband took his seat as the first Catholic member of parliament on 4 February 1830. For the next several years O'Connell focused his attention on parliamentary business carried out in London.

Although many historians consider this period during the 1830s to be 'the valley years in between the peaks of Emancipation and Repeal', the historian Donal McCartney argues that 'it is in this decade that the real O'Connell is revealed — the utilitarian pragmatist, the political opportunist'.[1] The following letters, therefore, which document a portion of this important juncture in O'Connell's career, are certainly valuable. But they allow much more than a glimpse at the life of an important political figure. Recent scholarship in the disciplines of family, social and women's history has revealed that personal letters such as these, which also detail the trivial and mundane matters of everyday life, are an essential source in our growing understanding of past times. The correspondence in this collection is thus doubly valuable. Found within its scope are insights into both the ordinary, though no less interesting, social history of the nineteenth century, as well as the extraordinary and exciting political history of parliamentary politics and the career of Daniel O'Connell.

On 9 May 1830 the fourteen-year-old Daniel O'Connell Jr[2] left his comfortable home in Merrion Square, Dublin. Following in the footsteps of his three older brothers, Danny was to begin his first term at Clongowes Wood College, a Jesuit-run boarding school located in County Kildare.[3] Danny was enrolled in Clongowes along with his very good friend Gregory Costigan.[4] The two boys were tested and placed in a rudimentary level from which Gregory was obviously promoted before Danny, much to the O'Connell family's dismay [7, 10].[5] Under the direction of its rector, Father B. Esmonde, the college curriculum embraced 'the full classical course adapted for universities, or learned professions: Hebrew (if required) — Italian — French — and English — with public speaking and composition — history — geography — writing — arithmetic — book-keeping — mathematics — philosophy and chemistry'. In addition to this wide range of subjects, the college boasted that 'Unceasing care is taken to convey to the minds of the pupils solid instructions on the principles of religion, and to engage their hearts to the observance of its precepts.'[6]

Despite this ambitious programme, extracts from Danny's journal reveal a somewhat dull and regimented lifestyle at the school:

> May the 11th. I got up this morning with the rest of the boys and went to Mr Fraser with Russel to find out what school Greg and I would be put. we were put into Rudiments. nothing of any consequence occurred for the rest of this day.

> May the 12th. We got our books to day and went down to Evening schools.

May the 13, 14, 15, 16, 17, 18, 19, 20, and all the days to the end passed over without any thing of serious consequence happening except that Gregory and I got the uniform.

June the 1st. We had very long prayers to day. We are beginning to dislike this place greatly.[7]

Study, exams and prayers made up the routine of most days, alongside meals, bathing and sport. Occasionally, as is wont to happen in an establishment full of young and energetic boys, less than scholarly events also occurred to break the daily monotony:

July 23rd . . . stones have been thrown in the Dormitory several times since I came here. they were thrown last night also . . .

July the 24th . . . I had a fight with a boy of the name of Jemmy M'carthy [of Cork] I shoved him a piece of paper with some thing written on it which he like a brat blotted. I caught a hold of his finger to make him let . . . it go. he began to skin me. we stopped soon for fear the prefect would catch us . . .[8]

The event most looked forward to, however, was the one-month vacation, granted each August. The days until its coming were painstakingly counted. 'Only *3 days and 17 hours of Vacation!!!! Hurra*,' wrote Danny on 29 July 1830. The eventual arrival of the long-awaited event brought excited shouts of joy, as Danny recorded on 2 August: 'I was awoke this morning by the boys shouting for Vacation . . . Vacation is at length arrived. Hurra, Hurra, Hurra. I am so very glad, hurra, Hurra Vacation for ever Hurra Hurra Hurra Hurra Hurra.'[9]

During the long days leading up to the break, letters from home served to ease the often lonely boarding-school routine. In Danny's case, his most prolific correspondent was his mother, Mary O'Connell. Bursting with motherly love and affection, and abounding in accounts of illness and death, politics and scandal, these letters, forty-seven of which are published here, allow a brief glimpse at the relationship between mother and son in nineteenth-century Ireland. As the nineteenth century progressed, maternal responsibilities gradually came to be seen as the means to a woman's fulfilment. Religious sentiment and educational philosophy began to emphasise the impressionability of a child's young mind, while Enlightenment psychology probed the connection between childhood influences and later adult characteristics. As a result, the essential role of the mother in moulding her offspring's character became a fundamental tenet of nineteenth-century thought on child-rearing and women's place in society. Motherhood, once merely a function of biological necessity, became an 'achieved status'.[10] The correspondence between Mary and her son, then, is relevant to our better understanding of what was, in the eyes of nineteenth-century society, one of the most important relationships a woman would ever have.

Unlike his brothers, who went away to school at about the age of seven, Danny junior studied at home until he turned fourteen. The reasons for this are unclear. Mary appears to have been slightly over-protective of her young son, and this may account for the choice to keep Danny at home. More likely, however, finances were to blame. At about the time Danny reached school age Mary and her children left Ireland for France in an attempt to live more economically. Although his brothers Morgan and John attended school, Mary taught Danny at home with help from his older sister Ellen. As a result, Mary's relationship with her youngest child was probably closer than most mother–son relationships of the day, allowing her greater influence over his actions. In fact Mary was, on more than one occasion, accused of spoiling the child. In 1820 Ellen O'Connell reported to her father: 'Mama says she whipped him [Danny junior] the other day but I don't think either you or I will attach much credit to that assertion.' She defended her mother, however, agreeing that Danny was such a 'bewitching little Darling and I don't wonder he should be a little spoiled'.[11]

Ellen's assessment was probably correct. Danny was Mary's baby, her youngest child, born six years after his brother John. In between these two boys, Mary had given birth to four other babies, all of whom died in infancy. It is no small wonder she doted upon the child. The entire family teased Mary about her favouritism towards her youngest son.

O'Connell commented at one stage that he was surprised she had let the nine-year-old child go to Ellen's home at Glencullen, County Wicklow, to stay the night. He did not think Mary could bear the separation and would worry with Danny so long out of her sight. Her response, voicing concern over Danny's riding habits, brought O'Connell's teasing reply, 'I quized you a little about Danny and you see I was right.' He admonished her to let the child jump his pony over ditches and even low walls, assuring her that Danny's seat was firm and that he was well able for such activity.[12] Still, Mary was sensitive to criticism regarding the upbringing of her children, and these letters attest to one occasion on which rumours of such criticisms reached her in Dublin [37].

Once the child entered Clongowes, however, Mary found her influence over her son weakened. The social constructs by which the masculine identity was formed frequently limited the relationship between a mother and her son. Women normally looked after both their male and female offspring until the boys were sent off to school, separated from females who remained at home. At school male headmasters, tutors and peers replaced a young boy's family as the centre of his life. This separation from women and children, which often allowed and even encouraged the denigration of women, was essential in shaping the male gender identity.[13] Mary found this to be true of her sons' experience at Clongowes. Each of the O'Connell boys entered the boarding school around the age of thirteen. 'What nice mannered boys Maurice and Morgan were when they went to Clongowes,' she observed in a letter to O'Connell. 'Indeed they may now well deny it. It is almost impossible to get them to divest themselves of the vulgarity they acquired at *that* college.'[14]

Yet Mary continued in her attempts to fulfil her motherly role, and her acceptance of the nineteenth-century ideal of motherhood is very apparent in her letters to her young son. Like other religious woman of her era, Mary believed her duty as a mother included ensuring the salvation of her offspring. She took great interest in Danny's religious activities while he was away at school. In particular, she demanded details regarding his first communion and frequently admonished him to pray, to attend mass and to offer up the sacrament for various intentions.[15] In addition, it was Mary's job as a mother to ensure that her child adopted the proper modes of speech and behaviour so important among the growing middle class. She pointed out errors in her son's letters and constantly admonished him regarding his personal appearance and hygiene [1, 7].

This attention to cleanliness gradually became a central focus of middle-class culture. Middle-class women, unlike their male counterparts, who found social power in owning property and associating with other men through business, charitable and political institutions, had few public arenas in which to amass power. Instead they were judged and judged others by the criteria of their modes of dress, their language, their manners and the way in which they kept their homes. Setting and enforcing proper standards of behaviour was one way in which a woman could influence and, in some small measure, hold power. Refusing to accept dirty hands, unwashed hair, muddy boots or vulgar speech allowed a woman some small degree of influence over her menfolk. Hence Mary's many entreaties to young Danny to keep clean. Even his sister Kate, six years older than her young brother, saw it her duty and place to exert her authority over Danny by insisting that he keep his hands and head clean [10].[16] Danny's aversion to washing, while somewhat repulsive to the modern reader, reveals nineteenth-century gender differences within the middle-class home where cleanliness and order were central tenets. Girls like Kate had to develop a dislike, even shame, of dirt as an expression of their femininity. Boys, on the other hand, were made to balance gentility with a manly disregard for such matters.[17] Danny, obviously, was still finding his way.

Mary's interest in Danny's cleanliness was just one example of her larger concerns over his general health and well-being. In reading through the correspondence, one is immediately struck by the amount of time devoted to sickness and health of writer, recipient, family and friends. A portion of nearly every letter confirms the well-being of its author, asks after the health of the recipient, and catalogues the status of all family members in relation to their physical fitness. The extent to which health is a dominant issue in the letters demonstrates the importance of good health in an era where physical well-being was fleeting at best. Indeed, a primary function of letter-writing was to ascertain or confirm the good health of the parties involved. Hence Mary insisted that Danny write to her or some other family member at least once every week. The constant and detailed attention to bodily functions, the frequent requests for descriptive accounts of aches and pains, the advice and directives to get well and stay well, the offhanded references to death, and the attentive surveillance of epidemic diseases all reveal a society obsessed with illness.

Cholera, for example, was greatly feared and was mentioned frequently in Mary's correspondence [30, 33, 36, 50, 53]. Arriving in Britain in 1831–32 from Asia or India, cholera was seen as a new and exotic disease which caused more extensive panic and had greater repercussions than other epidemic diseases such as fever, smallpox or tuberculosis. Cholera killed by dehydration. Death came very quickly, within three or four days, sometimes in only a few hours. The disease sparked widespread panic among all classes because it struck indiscriminately, wealthy or poor, young or old. It made its first appearance in Ireland in Belfast in March 1832 and appeared in Dublin one week later. By mid-April the disease was reported in Cork, and by May it had appeared in at least fourteen of the thirty-two counties. Those of means, such as the O'Connells, hoped to escape the plague by moving to safer environs, generally the countryside.[18]

Coming to terms with illness was only one function of letter-writing. It is worth noting that it fell mainly to Mary to maintain the correspondence between her family and her son. No letters from O'Connell to the young boy exist today; however, this collection cites O'Connell's many trips to Clongowes, while it documents only one visit from Mary. This 'division of labour' is symptomatic of the basic gender differences defining women's and men's roles in nineteenth-century Ireland. As the century progressed and the middle class grew, attempts were made to define people, places, time and matter by creating new categories, the most central being the distinction between the public arena and private sphere. Rules regarding social interaction and etiquette saw to it that the divisions between the public and private life of the middle classes became more marked. And gradually the partition between the home and the world was identified with gender. Women were increasingly bound to the private realm, while men could move between both spheres, holding influence in each.[19] In this instance, Mary, rooted firmly in her domestic sphere, conducted affairs from her writing-desk. Her limited power was filtered through her pen, her influence over her child diminished by distance, time and the constraints of etiquette. O'Connell, on the other hand, sallied forth into the world at his whim, visiting Danny in person, his very presence compounding his parental authority.

This is not to say, however, that Mary's letter-writing was ineffective. Often removed from her family and friends, she viewed letters as a life-line connecting her with the things that made her life full and worthy: her children, her husband and her extended family. The importance of letters can be seen in her many references to and complaints about their delay or non-existence. Indeed, a considerable portion of nearly every missive involved the actual mechanics of how one intended to send the letter, to which letter the current one replied, and the status of any letters received, unanswered or in transit. Mary was particularly exact in these details. Moreover, in her letters she made references to the many other people with whom she corresponded and the information which they imparted. The frequent appearance of second- and even third-hand information in the letters reveals the intricate network of family and friends whose amassed knowledge Mary redirected from her writing-desk to suit her own ends. From her pen flowed information, gossip, love and anger, by all of which she strove to bind her family together.

The letters published here reflect a period in which the O'Connell family was largely dispersed. Mary's letters to her youngest child began in the spring of 1830 while she was installed in London accompanied by her husband, her eldest child Maurice, and her daughters Kate and Betsey. Danny's brother Morgan, an officer in the Austrian service, was stationed on the continent, while his other brother, John, remained in Dublin to finish his studies at Trinity College. Ellen O'Connell, Danny's oldest sister, having married Christopher Fitz-Simon in 1825, was comfortably established in Ireland with two children and a third on the way.

The Irish political scene at this time was poised on the brink of change. In the past British rule in Ireland had been carried out through the parliament in Dublin. Since the end of the seventeenth century Catholics had been excluded from parliament as well as from other civil rights. Thereafter a series of penal laws were put into place which further restricted the liberties of the Catholic majority. During the eighteenth century, however, liberal elements within the Irish Protestant Ascendancy, influenced by more enlightened ideas, secured the relaxation of these penal laws and, in addition, called for even more freedom for their parliament in Dublin.

The outbreak of the French Revolution put a halt to these lofty aspirations. As liberalism grew more radical and ideas of patriotism began more closely to resemble Irish nationalism, the British government moved swiftly to save the Dublin parliament from possible takeover by a Catholic democracy. Thus, in 1800, the Irish parliament was abolished and Ireland was integrated into the United Kingdom to be ruled from the parliament at Westminster. The Church of England and the Church of Ireland became the one Protestant Episcopal Church of the United Kingdom.

The Union found support in many areas. Irish Protestants were willing to give up their parliament to ensure their ascendancy, to secure their religion, and to maintain their social dominance. Catholic landowners and middle-class professionals believed that their grievances would be more readily heard by a British government anxious to garner support for the Union. For the majority of Irish Catholics, Emancipation was of more importance than the Union; thus they were willing to concede to one parliament at Westminster.

Immediately after the enactment of the Union the Prime Minister, William Pitt, attempted to promote Emancipation, but his efforts met with staunch resistance from both George III and his cabinet. In Ireland, Protestant opposition to Catholic Emancipation was even more vocal. With the rise of Napoleon and fear of possible attack by the French, the issue of Emancipation became increasingly less important to parliament; as a result, Catholics saw their hopes diminishing. Catholic leaders met in November 1804 to establish a committee for the purpose of preparing and presenting to parliament a petition for the total abolition of the penal laws in Ireland. Daniel O'Connell took his place on that committee among peers and baronets, as a representative of the increasingly vocal middle-class lawyers and merchants. Catholic leaders had always been members of the landed gentry before 1792, when Catholics were first allowed to practise law. Gradually, however, the composition and style of the Catholic Committee began to change as these young and energetic middle-class lawyers moved to seize leadership.[20]

For Daniel O'Connell, Emancipation stood as a symbol of what was possible for Ireland. The advancement of the Irish Catholic, then, gradually became synonymous with the advancement of democracy, reform and improvement. By 1808 O'Connell had became the leader of the Emancipation movement. The Catholic Relief Act of 1829 finally allowed Catholics to make some inroads into the Protestant monopoly — allowing them access to the administration of government and law, positions in the police force and seats in parliament.[21]

Following Catholic Emancipation, the radical opinions of the day increasingly influenced the British parliament and encouraged parliamentary exertions in the area of reform. Having led the Catholics in their struggle for Emancipation, O'Connell was now certain that 'the benefits of good government had not reached the great mass of the Irish people, and could not reach them unless the Union should be either made a reality — or unless that hideous measure should be abrogated'. Convinced of the need to repeal the Act of Union, O'Connell began to campaign. Since an Irish legislature would bring benefits to all classes, the issue of Repeal joined together a large cross-section of Irish society, and as time passed it quickly gained widespread support.[22] It is here, in the year 1830, that our correspondence begins.

The year 1830 marked a formative time in British politics when one system of government was facing imminent demise and another was being created to take its place. As the nineteenth century progressed, the influence of Crown patronage in parliamentary power struggles was fast becoming a relic of eighteenth-century politics. For this reason, the 1828 by-election in County Clare, whereby Daniel O'Connell was elected as MP, seemed to signify the end of a parliamentary party system dominated by the Ascendancy. Political parties now found self-interest and family preservation were no longer issues on which to build a platform. Instead ideologies became the key factor in defining a party and amassing support. Moreover, between the years 1829 and 1845 both British politicians and the general populace began to realise that the affairs of Ireland were an integral part of British politics.[23] Although the future was uncertain, it was clear that some form of representative government would eventually be forthcoming. The supposed impending death of George IV added to the political uncertainty at this time and preoccupied political minds throughout the first half of 1830 [1, 2]. Because the monarch's death would incur a general election and a new parliament, both O'Connell and the House of Commons as a whole adopted a noncommittal stance on many issues. With the king's demise on 26 June, this period of hesitation finally came to an end [4].[24]

The popularity of O'Connell and his political agitation for Repeal posed a dangerous threat to the stability of British control in Ireland and led the government to act quickly against him. Henry William (Paget) first Marquess of Anglesey, who served as Lord Lieutenant of Ireland in the years 1828–29 and 1830–33, adopted a policy bent on thwarting O'Connell's Repeal movement. Between 26 December 1830 and 13 January 1831 he issued at least four proclamations suppressing all meetings relating to Repeal of the Union. His actions caused outrage among the masses and a decline in his own popularity. This outrage found public voice when Anglesey attended the theatre in Dublin on 12 January 1831. According to the *Freeman's Journal*, 'Upon taking his seat, a cheer was raised by the myrmidons of the Court, and of the police offices, which was joined in pretty generally — the anti-Unionists feeling a reluctance to insult a man whom they once had venerated: there were, however, very many hisses from the pit — the upper boxes and the galleries.'[25] Mary wrote to her son two days later of the incident and of the Lord Lieutenant's latest proclamation against Repeal meetings. Notwithstanding this turn of events, she informed Danny: 'your Father will contrive to have meetings' [7]. O'Connell had made this decision despite the arrest that very morning of the barrister and reluctant supporter of Repeal, Richard Lalor Sheil. O'Connell himself was not long to be spared.

On 18 January 1831 O'Connell and five of his lieutenants were arrested on thirty-one charges of conspiracy, seditious libel and unlawful assembly in direct violation of Anglesey's many proclamations. That night, released from custody, O'Connell spoke at the proceedings of a parochial meeting assembled to form a petition for the repeal of Anglesey's proclamations. Dubbing his arrest a 'Whig conspiracy to baffle the people', O'Connell claimed: 'The enemies of Ireland have dared to make a prisoner of me . . . a member of the House of Commons — they have done me the high honour to send a common thief-taker into my house, to arrest me in the sanctuary of my home — in the presence of the mother of my children.' The O'Connelite newspaper *The Pilot* of 19 January further reported that 'The arrests sanctioned by him who once earned the title of the "*beloved*," but may now be called the *besotted* Anglesey, have excited mixed sensations — of ridicule at their absurdity — and indignation at their despotism.' As Mary wrote to Danny of the public outcry resulting from his father's arrest, the Dublin papers reported that 'numerous groups of persons were seen collected in the streets earnestly discussing the circumstances attending this new indignity'.[26] Mary's, and later Kate's, account of O'Connell's arrest and the city's outrage against Anglesey [8, 9, 10, 11] adds an exciting flavour to the tale. Their descriptions of public agitation reveal the extent of O'Connell's popularity and support, as well as the significant threat he posed to the political *status quo*.

As the opening session of parliament drew near, Mary and her husband prepared to quit Ireland for London. Shortly before their departure, however, government officials sent word that O'Connell was not to leave the country. On 2 February 1831 *The Pilot* reported that despite the injunction against O'Connell's leaving Ireland, he had 'proceeded to Kingstown [Dún Laoghaire] as if he were proceeding to Parliament — got on board a steam packet, and when the vast assemblage had dispersed, returned in the evening. Thus he preserved the peace, and has done one more act entitling him to public gratitude.' According to the paper and Mary's letter to Danny [13], the procession accompanying O'Connell was some seven miles long, with an estimated crowd of 200,000. 'The vast multitude preserved admirable order — the splendour of the banners — the organization — the discipline, and almost military appearance of the different trades, had a most imposing effect,' reported *The Pilot*.[27]

As the trial drew near, accusations began to surface that O'Connell had entered into a compromise with the government to clear his name. On 14 February the Chief Secretary for Ireland, Edward Stanley, replied in parliament to a question regarding whether the government had made a deal with O'Connell in relation to his prosecution. Stanley stated that 'he was aware that an opinion had got abroad that O'Connell had pleaded guilty at the request of the government'. Although Stanley insisted that 'No such thing was the case', he did, however, intimate that friends of O'Connell had been 'endeavouring to effect a compromise'. O'Connell responded to the matter on 28 February, declaring that he had authorised no one to attempt a compromise on his behalf, thus contradicting what Mary described as Stanley's 'lying statement' [16, 17].[28] In any event, O'Connell's trial was postponed, and the Liberator was finally allowed to leave Ireland and take his seat in parliament. O'Connell's supporters rejoiced, and, according to Mary, when this piece of good news reached his native town of Cahirciveen, County Kerry, 'the town was illuminated and the country in a *blaze* with lampires' [16]. By May the Whigs, needing O'Connell's backing for their Reform Bill, dropped the charges against him, citing the expiration of the Proclamation Act under which he was charged.

Since the issue of Repeal was wholeheartedly rejected by the Tories and found little support from the Irish or Catholic Whigs, O'Connell changed his tactics. Although he still found Repeal to be ultimately preferable, he conceded to reform. Once he had taken his seat in parliament, O'Connell was particularly intent upon reforming the electoral and representative system which essentially allowed the landed aristocracy to control nearly every seat in parliament. To this end, he gave his support to the reforming radicals who belonged to no party. O'Connell too was a radical reformer who supported triennial parliaments, male suffrage, a secret ballot and an elective House of Lords. He frequently addressed the house three or four times daily on these issues throughout the session.[29]

Thus, as parliamentary reform became the dominant issue of the 1831 session, O'Connell joined the movement. With a trial no longer looming, O'Connell was able to return to the House of Commons in time to speak in favour of the Reform Bill presented to parliament on 1 March 1831. Although the bill was defeated, O'Connell's support of reform marked his new alliance with the Whig government. 'You cannot conceive what change there is already towards me in the House,' he wrote to Mary regarding this new affiliation.[30]

The spring of 1831 also saw O'Connell embroiled in a general election. From London Mary watched its progress, sending reports to her son at Clongowes. On 14 May O'Connell was returned for Kerry, the Knight of Kerry having resigned. In Clare, James O'Gorman Mahon put himself up as a candidate against O'Connell's son Maurice. Returned for Clare the previous August, O'Gorman Mahon was later found guilty of bribery during the election and had been replaced by Maurice O'Connell on 23 March 1831 [19]. Now the two candidates faced each other again, and the campaign soon turned dirty. The first attack came from *The Pilot* when its editors alleged that O'Gorman Mahon had allied himself with the Terry Alts, an agrarian secret society active in Clare. The *Freeman's Journal*, however, dismissed the accusation as an 'unfounded allegation' and 'malicious invention'.[31] Next, according to *The Pilot*, William Mahon, brother of O'Gorman Mahon, directed a 'wanton insult' towards Maurice O'Connell, 'which ended as most affairs where gross insult is offered, in the peaceable conduct of the person offending, when time and the pistol's mouth give cool reflection'. Mahon apparently hurled the insult 'without provocation or pretence . . . in order to intimidate, or end the election'. Maurice, upon winning the seat, sought satisfaction from Mahon in the form of a duel. Difficulty in finding an appropriate location in which to hold the affair, however, resulted in the event never taking place.[32] Despite this peaceful outcome, the affair obviously caused Maurice's mother some worry [27].

With the election safely won, O'Connell continued to promote the Reform Bill throughout 1831. The second bill had been passed in the Commons in July, but the Lords defeated it in October. O'Connell's promotional activities led him, in January 1832, to Wolverhampton, where the Political Union had invited him to accept an address [46]. On the following day he journeyed on and, at the Birmingham Political Union, spoke to a crowd of reportedly 15,000 to 20,000 people. In his speech he declared his support for the English Reform Bill; however, he also demanded a Reform Bill for Ireland equal to that about to be voted in for England.[33]

Presented by Earl Grey, the Reform Bill finally passed by nine votes on 14 April 1832. The bill allowed for an alliance between parliament's liberal element and those promoting Catholic democracy. This alliance, in turn, toppled the Tories, whose platform had dominated parliamentary politics since the Union. To O'Connell, however, the bill was sadly lacking. He had hoped that any reform would increase Irish representation and lower the qualifications for the franchise. Although the bill increased the number of electors, O'Connell found it to be too conservative and lacking in uniformity. There was no disfranchisement, only five seats were conceded, and the franchise qualifications were set so high that no transfer of the electoral power in the constituencies would be possible.[34]

Disappointed at this outcome, O'Connell once again turned his attention to Repeal, making it a key issue in the general election of 1832. He had returned to Dublin in early March, leaving his son Maurice to deal with an important debate in parliament on the tithe question.[35] Busying himself with both legal engagements and a popular campaign in Munster, O'Connell promoted his Repeal party throughout Ireland [51]. 'I would not join in any violation of the Law,' declared O'Connell. 'My plan is to restore the Irish Parliament with the full assent of Protestants and Presbyterians as well as Catholics. I desire no social revolution, no social change . . . In short, salutary restoration without revolution, an Irish Parliament, British connection, one King, two legislatures.'[36] When the general election took place in December 1832, O'Connell's Repeal party took 39 seats, 26 of these being held by Catholics. His sons Maurice, Morgan and John, his son-in-law Christopher Fitz-Simon and his brother Nicholas, as well as a brother-in-law and a cousin, all won seats, creating a strong party core. Yet many party members and their supporters were not strong Repealers; Emancipation and reform had won them their seats. When the issue of Repeal was tested by a vote in the Commons in 1834, it was soundly defeated. Hence, from this time forward, O'Connell set his sights on 'good government' rather than 'home government'.[37]

Danny remained at Clongowes for two years. As the letters attest, O'Connell purchased a partnership in Madder's Brewery — later renamed O'Connell's Brewery — in 1831 for his youngest son. It was hoped that Danny would take over the running of the brewery upon his coming of age. Founded in 1788 by an Englishman named Samuel Madder in partnership with John and Paul Patrick, and known as Phoenix Brewery, the operation made its home in James's Gate near its rival Guinness's Brewery. The enterprise had been plagued with debts for several years owing to an overambitioius expansion project and had changed hands a number of times before O'Connell acquired it.[38]

It is likely that O'Connell's foray into brewing was meant to subsidise his politics. Indeed, Mary's letters suggest that drinking 'the real Dan' was a sure sign of one's political persuasion and loyalty to her husband's cause. She often mentions both O'Connell's growing popularity and the success of the porter in the same sentence [35, 39, 51]. However, neither Danny, then only fifteen, nor any of his partners knew anything of running a business; nor were they versed in the art of brewing. Despite Mary's enthusiastic predictions of its success, and John O'Connell's praise for the quality of the porter [37, 39, 47], the firm did not prosper. In fact the brew was usually unsaleable. In 1832 John Brenan, a qualified brewer, attempted to rescue the failing operation. He invested heavily in the enterprise, but to no avail. By 1840 the brewery had foundered, and the O'Connells' connection with it ended in 1841.[39]

Not surprisingly, Danny junior eventually became an MP, representing Dundalk 1846–47, Waterford City 1847–48, and Tralee 1853–63. In 1863 he removed to London to take up the post of Commissioner of Income Tax. In 1867 he married Ellen Mary Foster, with whom he had ten children. Daniel O'Connell Jr died in 1897.[40]

After 1832 Mary and her husband were hardly ever separated; hence correspondence between the two became less frequent. As a result, information regarding Mary's activities and private life during her later years is lacking. She travelled a great deal with her husband, whose political career kept him moving between Ireland and England at regular intervals. Gradually, however, Mary's continued ill-health caught up with her. Surviving correspondence suggests that her decline began in September 1835. Yet she continued to travel between Kerry, Dublin and London, which in some measure suggests a recovery. In May 1836 she began taking the waters at Tunbridge Wells in Kent, which were believed to be the best for her unknown 'complaint'. By August Mary and Daniel had returned to the family home in Derrynane, where Mary's health continued to deteriorate. She lingered until 31 October 1836, and was buried on the Abbey Island at Derrynane.[41]

Mary O'Connell, like many of her contemporaries, was a prolific writer. Although she once confessed to Danny, in reference to letter-writing, 'I hate it' [27], she was not deterred from putting pen to paper on at least 315 known occasions in order to keep in touch with her ever-dispersed family. Making up a substantial part of the O'Connell correspondence housed in the National Library of Ireland, the extant letters represent only a very small portion of what she must have written during her lifetime. The majority of the following fifty-three letters were written to Danny at Clongowes. Forty-seven are from Mary, while two letters each appear from John and Kate O'Connell to their younger brother. In addition, James O'Connor, Danny's schoolmaster, provides a single missive to the boy's mother.

Unfortunately only one letter from Danny to his mother survives. Much to Mary's frequent dismay, Danny was not as consistent a correspondent as she would have liked. She often admonishes him in this collection to write to her more regularly. Her distress at not receiving mail from her son was no family secret. John O'Connell, obviously a witness to his mother's suffering, even took it upon himself to encourage Danny to 'write more regularly than you do' to their mother [6]. During one particularly long silence Mary, worried that Danny might have fallen ill, confessed her fears to her husband. O'Connell, a rather irregular correspondent himself, dismissed her fears as groundless. If Danny was ill, O'Connell, wrote, the Jesuits at Clongowes would send word. 'Besides,' he concluded somewhat condescendingly, 'you have no idea of the rapidity with which time flies over at a school where everything is done like clockwork.'[42] In the end Mary's unease was justified. Danny had been ill with a cold which also affected his eyes and prevented him from writing home [14].

Editorial Note

Generally the letters in this collection are well written and require no clarification. Mary, however, rarely used any punctuation; nor did she bother to capitalise the first letter of a sentence. Thus punctuation and capital letters have been added to aid the reader. Mary also randomly capitalised letters within a sentence, as well as underlining certain words, sometimes for no apparent reason. These oddities have been retained. In addition, while her spelling is relatively good, Mary was lax in using a consistent spelling for proper names. Thus Ellen's home in Ballinemena, County Wicklow, might appear as both *Ballenemena* and *Ballinamena* in the same letter; similarly, the name of Danny's school chum Gregory Costigan appears in several versions. Even Mary's own daughter is not immune, for *Betsey* and *Betsy* are used interchangeably. Lastly, Mary never used an apostrophe to mark possession or when using a contraction. For example, in referring to *O'Connell's speech*, Mary would write *O'Connells speech*; her spelling of *can't* would be *cant*. These quirks are also retained unless the misspelling might result in confusion to the reader.

Occasional explanatory interpolations are placed within square brackets; missing letters or words are also included within square brackets. Where there is doubt concerning the reading of a particular word or phrase, a bracketed question mark has been added. Tears in the manuscripts resulting in loss of text are represented by angled brackets, thus: < . . . >.

O'Connell Family Letters, 1830–1832

[NLI, MSS 13644–5; NLI, microfilm P. 1621]

1. *Mary O'Connell to Daniel O'Connell Jr*

Maddox Street [London]
Saturday [22 May 1830]

My darling Danny

It was a great pleasure to me this morning to get your first letter from Clongows but I will not allow you to address [me] by any appellation but that of Mod. You are much improved in your writing but you ought to attend to your spelling. There are three words badly spelt. Instead of office you wrote *offiece*, and you wrote *Munday* instead of Monday. Instead of friends you wrote freinds and oenly when it should be only — you dont tell me what Class you are in at what hour you go to bed and get up and if you are studying so as to save the year. When are you to make your first Communion. Who is your Director and what is your Number at school. I wish to know every particular. We are all well and merry.

Last evening we were at Astleys where I saw such a Poney as your Jack Pass and go through various feats in the Circus. The Girls told me when I was wishing for you that you had seen such an entertainment at Adams and at Duncranes in in Dublin.

We had a letter this post from Ellen.[1] She and her babes are well. So is John.[2] Your Father will probably go to see you when he goes to Dublin next Month. When you write to me always desire your love particularly to your *Fath*.

I had a letter from Mamma B [Mary's mother] yesterday. She desired her love to her favourite Danny. Morgan[3] is now at Grena quite well. Maurice Bemman is to be immediately married to a Miss Power of Cork. Would you like to get a Dublin newspaper. If you wish for one I should send a paper very regularly.

Your Father had a letter from Mr L'Estrange[4] from Rome. He is quite recovered but does not speak of coming home. The chapels here (they dont deserve to be called churches) are very few and small. The Chapel at Chelsea is the only good chapel I have seen. Yet the Superior of it is a french Abbe. He reminded me of poor Mr Verge. We go on

Sunday week to hear Mass at Moorfield Chapel. I heard a Sermon last Sunday from an Irish Priest. It was quite a treat to our ears. It was for the Catholic charity school belonging to the Chelsea Hospital which is principally supported by the french Abbe. There were a number of the old Pensioners at Mass several of them Irish Men.

Maurice[5] does not leave until we are going I believe next month. They say the King may live for six Months more. I shall my darling Danny count the days until I have the happiness of embracing you. Tell Greg [Costigan] I will have a nice Poney for him. I hope Mrs Costigen will go to see you soon. Your Fath Maurice and the Girls unite in love to you with my darling child your ever fond Mother

Mary Ô Connell

The Girls desire their love to Greg. Your friend Mr. Hurt [Hunt?] has left London. I dare say you will have a visit from him. Johnny mentions to day that Charles Henry and Henry FitzSymon were going down to see you. Hanna and James [family servants] desire their love. John is trying to pick up the English *accent*.

2. *Mary O'Connell to Daniel O'Connell Jr*

Maddox Street [London]
Monday [31 May 1830]

My darling child

I got your letter written yesterday week and am happy to tell you *there* are *now* but 63 days to Vacation. Before that period arrives I hope you will have distinguished yourself at school and bring a premium home.

The King is very ill. They do not expect he will survive many days. Our stay is uncertain but we hope to be in Ireland the latter end of June.

I heard this day from Johnny. He is well. We heard on Saturday from Morgan. He was then at Grena greatly delighted with all the hunting he has had. He says Stranger [Danny's dog] is quite well and has killed another Rat one of 'the Elephant species.' He is not as fat as he was. Jack darling is quite gay. I shall take care to have a Poney for Greg and Mick Kelly to attend you both.

Ricarda [Connor, Danny's cousin] is to be married next Sunday. She goes in two days after to Killgrave. Betsey Leyne [cousin] is to go there during the summer with her Aunt Ellen and they will pay us a visit to the Abbey. But I fancy Mary Anne and Bessy will not.

We met in the park yesterday O Gorman Mahon and his Wife and her sister in a very nice green chariot with post horses and two servants in green behind. We had a salute from Mrs Mahon but *he* did not presume to salute us. We have very bad weather here which prevents us from seeing many places.

Ellen is at Ballinamena. She mentions to day that Mary is in the greatest delight with all the live *stock* there. She knew Mrs Heely and the other people quite well. John intends going for a few days to Ballinamena. He is jealous with you for not writing to him. Maurice begs to tell you with his love your boat will be in great order before you. Tom O Connell is filling it up. He is now at the Abbey. Your Father is is in good health though he goes through a good deal of fatigue. I never was better. When I see anything that I think you would enjoy seeing I always wish for you. Indeed you are seldom from my thoughts. Your sisters often speak of you so does your *Fath* and Maurice.

When are you to go to Communion. Let me know exactly are you yet able to answer Mass. Kate[6] had a letter from Mr L'Estrange last week from Rome. He beged to be kindly remembered to you and Greg. Charles Connor will be our chaplain this summer at the Abbey. Do you get tea at breakfast and in the morning. Are you ever sick. God bless you my darling child with love from your *Fath* and the Girls. Believe me your fond Mother.

Mary Ô Connell

Remember all of us to Greg. Consolments to Mr Esmond [schoolmaster]. James and Hanna beg their love to you. You are a great favourite to each of them. How are the Russells [schoolmates]. Remember me your sisters and Maurice to them. How is their Father and their Mother and where are they.

3. *Mary O'Connell to Daniel O'Connell Jr*

Friday Morning [4 June 1830]

My darling Danny

I got your letter written on the 31st this morning and am much pleased with the answers you give to all my questions. Now to answer your questions. In the first place I am most anxious that you should go to Communion on the 21st of this month it being the feast of St Alloysius the Patron saint of your college. It was on that day that each of your brothers made their first Communion. Tell your director my wish on the subject but let him as the most proper Person decide the matter. I beg of you my darling child to give your mind to your studies. You have been too long idle and consider the pleasure it would give your good Father and how much happier you will feel coming home at Vacation. I send you this day two Freemans Journals. Betsey[7] will inclose you a long letter. With love from your Fath. Believe me ever your fond *Mod*.

Mary Ô Connell

4. *Mary O'Connell to Daniel O'Connell Jr*

Saturday July the 3d [1830]

My dearest Danny

After many days of great anxiety at your long silence I had the happiness to receive your letter of the 29th this morning. Why my dear child are you so careless about writing. Surely it is not too much for your Mod to expect a letter every week from Danny who used to be fond of her and not ashamed to call her *Mod*. Your brothers who are much older than you always address me in their letters by the appellation of Mod. Wont you in future do the same.

Your Father and I are much disappointed you have not made your first Communion on St Aloysius Day or since that day more particular as Anne Costigan mentioned to Kate that Doctor Murphy told her you were at Communion on the Patron Saints day of the Jesuits. I trust my child the delay is not occasioned by your neglect or foolish scruples. May God give you grace to make a good Communion when you are allowed to go.

The Vacation is fast approaching. Have you any chance at premium. As usual your brother John got no premium at his first or last examination. This you may suppose annoys your Father greatly. He said to me the other morning 'I hope our Danny will not be idle. He will get premiums for his Father.' Let this my child stimulate you to do all in your power to get even one premium.

This Vacation John is gone to Kerry. We shall leave for Ireland on Monday week. I will write to you again before we start and let you know how you are to travel. You have heard of the Kings death. He is to be interred next Thursday. Your Father will go from here to Dublin. We shall go from Bristol to Cork and so on to Kerry.

I had a letter the other day from your Mama B. She desired twenty loves to you. James Conner is quite recovered. Betsey Leyne is gone home but will I believe return to her Aunt Ellen in a month. Ricarda Primrose is as happy as possible. She goes to the Killarney races. We shall be too late for them. I suppose you have heard that Miss Margret Shiel is to be married this month to Mr Kenley [?]. Tell Gregory I shall have a green ribbon for him. She has been as faithless to him as Mrs FitzSymon [Danny's sister, Ellen O'Connell Fitz-Simon] was. 'Alas poor Gregory.'

We went to see Keane[8] on last Friday Night week in Shylock. He was very great. Your Father surprised us at the conclusion of the fourth act by walking into the box. He stopped until we were all going and was much amused at the after piece 'the happiest day of my life'. Your Father came to us from the house of Commons there not being a sufficient number of Members to have any debate.

We are very anxious to get out of London. It is becoming so stupid. I believe the Mahons are gone. Mahon is <deter>mined to stand for Clare. Your Father will certainly be returned for some County. He has many offers. Thank God he is quite well though he goes through great fatigue. The late hours are shocking. He is now going to bed when formerly he used to be getting up. Maurice is very well very anxious to get on board his Yacht which is by this time quite ready for him. Morgan is I believe still in Iveragh hunting every day and dancing every Night. John is to stop with Roger Sullivan until after the Races. Dan is still in Dublin.

Saturday Night. This letter will go by the post of tomorrow and I hope you will write to me at once. I leave on Monday week and your letters I never get until the fifth day after they are written. If you write the day after you get this letter I shall get your answer before I leave on Monday the 12th. Hanna and James are greatly obliged for your remembrance of them. They beg to be kindly remembered to you. Love to Gregory. Good Night Love.

5. *Mary O'Connell to Daniel O'Connell Jr*

Merrion Square
Monday [3 January 1831]

My darling Danny

I beg your pardon for thinking for one moment that any cause save sickness alone would prevent you from writing to your Mother who loves you if possible more than ever for the good sense you have shown in bearing your disappointment of not spending this Christmas at home. I am truly delighted you were so merry. I cant say we had much merriment here. You had believe me no less and you have now to look forward to the happiness of seeing your dear Father next Saturday to stop until Monday should it be no inconvenience to Mr Esmond or the other Gentlemen. Your Father is delighted at your getting first in composition. He has ordered the fluted skates for you and will take them to you with the candles letter paper and Christmas prog[9] from me. Maurice and Morgan will accompany your Father on Saturday.

You dont say my Child if you have been as yet to Communion. Should you not go on Thursday next for mercys sake be prepared to go next Sunday Morning with your Father who will certainly go in the

Chapel at Clongows. He will be unhappy as well as myself until you have fulfilled your Christmas duty.

I thought I should never get a letter from you. The one I got to day was written on Friday last. I hope you will have more weather for skating. I enjoyed the frost and snow very much for your sake.

No news in Dublin only your Father is a greater Man in Ireland than my Lord Anglessy. No news from the Country. Your Maid [former wet-nurse] Nancy and her husband Paddy Doyle are in Town. They enquired very kindly for you. They have got four children.

Do you get wild fowl. Let me know if you think Mr Esmond would like some for next Sunday and I shall send him some by your Father. Had you any theatricals this Christmas. I am near writing in the dark and I cant get a frank. We heard to day from Ellen. She and the babes are quite well. There was a letter from Mr L'Estrange the other day. He is in tolerable health and will be home in Spring. This day three months will be Easter Sunday. Good by my darling Child. With love from your Father your brothers and sisters.

> your fond Mother
> Mary Ô Connell

love to Gregory
all his family are well

I never see the Coffys or the Hearns [family friends] in the street. I paid Frank Henry for his loss of the Trousers. His Father is in England. His Mother was very ill the other day. Charles and Frank are to go to the school immediately to the Rock. John got your letter and will attend to your directions about the fluted skaits. He will soon write to you. Once more good by.

6. *John O'Connell to Daniel O'Connor Jr*

Thursday [6 January 1831]

My dear *Imperator primus*

Mama wishes you to tell Revd Mr Esmond that my father will be down to *dinner* on Saturday & remain till Monday *if allowed*. She has sent

you the candles by Hardwick Street. The skates &c. &c. will be brought
down to you by my father. She bids you take care of the skates as they
cost fifteen shillings. I chose them at Lamprey's, so you may be sure of
the goodness of the material. They are of walnut wood & fluted. By the
bye, if you wanted to skate well, the plain skate is the sort you should
have but as there never is in Ireland, much opportunity for the amuse-
ment, the fluted skates will answer every purpose of yours. I am glad
you have taken a fancy to skating. I was very fond of it although I skated
very badly. I have told Mamma to send you down a gimlet also to bore
your shoes with, they were great *desiderata* in my day.

When you are directing a letter next, put the name of the person (to
whom you write) without any 'For' or 'To' before it. No one puts
either of those words now upon the address of their letters, it is old
fashioned to do so.

We had a party/dinner & evening here, last Tuesday, but as Kate
wrote to you yesterday, I shall not give you an account of it as I suppose
she gave it in detail. I am writing this in a great hurry it being past
twelve & I having to go to mass.

I got a letter from Maurice Ô Connor (the Doctor) [cousin] today,
it is the second he has written me from Edinburgh. He is very well but
is extremely dissatisfied with the good people of the town & the Scotch
in general. His epistle is little more than a tirade against them. James,
his brother, was up here, as you must have heard, last term. He returns
early in February.

Dublin is very stupid at present, no parties & no public amusements
but the theatre. The latter, under Calcrafts management, & belonging
to himself, is getting on much better than it has done for some years.
However, I am afraid that the poor fellow will be ruined by the specu-
lation, like all his predecessors. He deserves support as he spares no
effort to please.

Your friends the Hearnes & Coffeys are very well, I see them frequently. Marty took your letter last night to Edward Hearne. Write
more regularly than you do to Mamma, you have no idea how much
it frets her when she does not hear from you in due course. She is

actually miserable. Greg's people are all quite well. Give my love to him. Send me word in your next letter to Mamma, where Henry Russell is, if in Derbyshire or London. Neddy will tell you. I want to write to him while I have my father here to frank for me.[10]

I congratulate you on your having distinguished yourself. Endeavour next term to get first in Examen. Nothing is of greater use to a person. It is in fact, the true way of getting first in compositions afterwards.

I shall not give you any politics as you are going to have my father down, who will tell you every thing that is to be told. I must hasten to a conclusion as it is getting very late. All here send their love to you. Poor James is not very well but that is no new thing with him. The Harry's are all quite well, Susan is still *faithful*. Old Harry is gone to England to take the office of Lord Chancellor.[11] Their new house is not half so large as their former one at Johnstown, but it is within half the distance from town. Stranger is quite well & sends his best respects. Believe me dear Danny

your truly fond brother
John D'Evreux Ô Connell

7. *Mary O'Connell to Daniel O'Connell Jr*

Merrion Square
Friday Morning [14 January 1831]

My darling Child

At lenght my eye is well enough to allow me to write to you. The skates I have not got as yet but when I do I shall try to get them exchanged for a larger size.

Your Father and the boys arrived at home at half past one O Clock last Monday quite delighted with their trip to Clongows. Your Father told me your hair and your hands were filthy both days. Did you not my Child promise me you would be particular in keeping your head combed and your person clean. But when you neglected to do so on those two days your neglect in other days must be dreadful. I tremble to think what the consequence will be of neglecting to comb and clean your head. You will get ring worms in your head and John has assured me he has seen boys in such a state from neglect of the head as to have it. One M[*illegible*] of [*illegible*] with a running sore on the neck proceding him the worms. Let me implore of you to neglect your head no longer. The weather is now mild enough for you to get your hair trimmed and then you can the more easily keep your head combed. A boy in the 15th year of his age to be obliged to be spoken to to keep himself clean. When Maurice was coming away Mr Shine beged to speak to him about you. He said you were quite fit for the second school as Gregory Costigin but that you had taken it into your head it is not necessary to learn much latin at school as you were to come home in two years and to have then a tutor. Now my Child you must recollect you were expressly told that if you made good use of your time while these two years are passing you would be brought home at their termination. Are you aware that it is a resident tuter you are to have. One who will go with you to the Country. That the Classics are what you are entirely to learn from him to fit you for entering College. Now my dear Danny will it not be better for you to make every exertion while at Clongows to learn as much of the Classics as you possibly can. If you will take a little more trouble you can do any thing because you have abilitys and surely you ought to be at least in the same class with Gregory. You are my darling Child, religious and conscientious. Surely you will not commit so much sin as to neglect studying and doing all in your power to repay your good Father for the expense he is at for you. I am sure I need not urge you more on this subject. You love the Mother who loves you in her heart and you will by studying closely at present give her the happiness of having you at home at the end of two years. Get into the school with Gregory without delay. Let him not be above you in any way.

You will be sorry to hear poor Pat Doyle is dead. He went to bed as well as possible the other evening, complained of being ill in the Night. Nancy [Doyle's wife and Danny's former wetnurse] got up to light the Candle. When she came back he was speechless and lived but a few moments after. Poor Mrs Kinley is also dead. Miss Esmond was married last week to a Mr Locke a Man of large fortune. Perthey Kelly is immediately to be married to Miss Mahon. Poor Aunty Nagle is dangerously ill.

Mr Shiel was this morning arrested for a speech of his made at one of the meetings. Maurice went to the Police office to give bail for him. The Marquis has this day published written proclamation against all meetings however your Father will contrive to have meetings. The Marquis is annoyed because he was so hissed at the other Night at the Theatre.

I gave Mr. Nicholson[12] your letter. He gave me mass this morning. He is to have a consultation of Doctors to day about his health. He is very nervous. All our friends in Kerry are very well. I sent Nancy a crown *from* you with one from myself to help to bury her husband. I also gave her other help for your sake.

Did you like the prog I sent you. I thought it was as good and as what Gregory got. Did you like the beef and the rasberry vinegar. I spoke to Julia to to write to you. She has been complaining. Poor Kate has been suffering with a toothache. She is gone to day to get it drawn.

[*remainder missing*]

8. *Mary O'Connell to Daniel O'Connell Jr*

Merrion Square
Wednesday [19 January 1831]

Love to Gregory. Your Uncle Finns dog Bill has yet <u>seven</u> *Grand children* born yesterday 'I fancy I would be able to beat Mrs Costigan on the *rail*'

My Darling Child

Since I last wrote to you I had the happiness of seeing dearest Ellen and her babes. Your Father and I accompanied by your brothers and sisters and Mr. Nicholson went down on Saturday to Ballinamena and stopped until Monday. Mary [Danny's niece, dauther of Ellen O'Connell Fitz-Simon] was in the greatest delight to see us but she did not forget to ask for Unty Danny. She is a dear little thing. Speaks now quite plain and hums little Nursery verses which she repeats so prettily. I will at the other side give you a copy of some of them. O'Connell [Danny's nephew] is weaned. He is a fine Creature very like your brother John when at his age. He does not say many words merely Dada and Mama. *Sissy* which Mary taught him by great perseverance and Aunt *tate* [i.e. Kate] of whom he is very fond. Christy [another nephew] is a lovely fine Infant.

You will have great pleasure with them next Summer at the Abby. Probably you will be going down to Cork in the same Steam packet. By that mode they mean to *travel* to Cork. Ballenamena as it is no longer to have house added to it is very much improved. However I would prefer their living at Glencullen. Tom FitzSimon has given it up to O Mara. He has taken a farm in the Queens County. We know nothing of the O Maras.

I heard from Mama B the other day. She is quite well and desired her fondest love to you. Aunt Chute is quite recovered. Bess Leyne has got a young son. I fancy it will be called Daniel Ô Connell Leyne. Did I tell that Charles O Connor has got a bursary in England worth him a £1010 a year. He is greatly pleased with England. James is still at Cove. Your poor Aunt Nagle was very near dying. She is now out of all danger. All our other Kerry friends are well. Mrs O Donoghue is recovered from the Measles. Bric is in *good health*. *Gabby* is to be married as soon as she has her *Catechism* in English to a farmers son in Iveragh. She gets £20 fortune from your Uncle James. Ally is a great housekeeper at Derrinane. She always mentions that Jack is very well.

You will see in the Pilot of this night an account of your Fathers being arrested yesterday morning by the orders of Lord Anglessy. Thank God it is out of his power to hurt him. Pray my child for your Father and for your brothers. If your Father had gone to Newgate yesterday the Castle would have been torn down last Night the people were so indignant.[13] Thank God he is able to keep them quiet. He was this morning presented with a handsome silver chased cup with a cover on it by the Committee of the Orphan charity society and a beautiful address also an orange and Green cloth cap by the Cap Makers. How proud you ought to be of such a Father and how anxious to gratify him by close attention to your studys and keeping your person clean.

Why dont you write to me. Nothing new here. Dublin never was so stupid. We have not been at any party this Winter. Mr Esmond is in the county Waterford. You will soon have him at home. With fondest love from your Father Sisters and brothers. Believe me my dear child ever your fond

Mother Mary Ô Connell

[*Postscript contains two nursery rhymes*]

9. *Mary O'Connell to Daniel O'Connell Jr*

Saturday Morning [January 1831]

My dearest Danny

Eight days yesterday since I had the favour of a line from you. Were it not for Gregory who mentions you in his letter this week I should indeed be uneasy though I trust there exists no cause but your fault of putting off until tomorrow what ought to be done to day. Let me again implore of you to write at least once in every week to me or to some Member of your family.

Your Father is thank God in spite of his *friend* the Marquis quite well. Since his arrest there have been many others which you have I suppose read of in the Pilot. The Marquis is now as much disliked as he was before liked, and his arrest of your Father has got many friends for the repeal of the Union. Before this time next year we shall God willing have a parliament of our own.

Mr Nicholson gave us Mass this Morning. He goes this day by the advice of his Physicians to the Country for a few weeks to Maire O Farrells. I should not be at all surprised if he paid you a visit. He is very delicate.

Kate had a letter last week from Mr L'Estrange. He is quite well. Will be home in Spring. Mr Whelan was ill this week. He is now much better. Sylvester Gastigan [*Costigan*] is going to Scotland on some Mercantile business. I suppose you read in the Pilot that Mr O Loghlin is made a

Sergeant at Law. He told me the other day he had a great rise out of his son Hugh by telling him Dan O Connell was arrived 'clasping his hands he cried out oh Papa is he come back from school. I am so very glad.'

[*remainder torn off and missing*]

10. *Catherine (Kate) O'Connell to Daniel O'Connell Jr*

Merrion Square
January 26th 1831

My dear Danny.

Mama got both your letters. She desires me say that my Father is quite against your learning the flute for the present as he is more anxious that you should attend to your latin & indeed my dear Boy I think it will give you enough to do. Do you remember the song you had when a little fellow. Y was a youth who walked in the Park and played on the flute till he made the dogs bark. My father advises you to beware of his example, the only thing they wish you to learn extra is fencing which would be of much use to you. When you return to school after the summer vacation you may learn the flute if you like.

Mama desires me say too, that she thinks it a great shame for you not to be in the same class with Greg, you ought to work hard & get away from the little boys you are with. Consider it is no honor to be first amongst such little fellows. What is easy to you is difficult to them. When my Father went to school in france he was put into the first class in every thing but in french which of course he knew very badly & all the others in the class had been in the country for years & were quite french-men. He worked so hard that in six months he was second in french. What say you to that? Mama was also very glad to hear that you had got yr. hair cut. I hope it is quite close the way Greg's was. For charity sake my dear boy be careful in combing it. I assure you if you don't you'll get a horrid *sore* head & you won't be able to get rid of it for months. I hope you wash yr. hands at least every morning. If you don't give yourself this habit now you won't be able to be clean when you are at home.

All friends in Kerry are quite well. Phrey was very ill for some days but is now recovered. Alicia is still in Cork & very gay. We expect Ellen, Fitz, Mary & Christie to town to day to see my Father before he goes away.

I dare say you will have heard before you get this that the bills were found against my Father & the others. You can't think how Lord Anglesey is hated. They hooted [?] him the other day & filled his < . . . > with mud. The people are quite < . . . > agitation. They follow my Father in thousands & he has to speak to them every night from the balcony. He is quite well thank God & in excellent spirits.

Mama desires me tell you she fears they won't exchange your skates as no agreement to that effect was made with them & besides your name is written on them. She will try however & if not she will send them back to you as you seem to have some chance of wanting them if this weather continues.

Mrs. Costigan & the girls were just here & desire their love to Greg & you in which my dear Dan all here unite with

your fond Sister

Kate

Mama did send yr letter long since to Alley

11. *Mary O'Connell to Daniel O'Connell Jr*

Merrion Square

Sunday [January 1831]

I spoke to Julia. She told me she would write to you yesterday. She and the *little* Admirale are very well and very merry.

My dearest Danny

You mistook the fair part of Kates letter. Your Father and myself had an objection to your learning the flute until you become a Member of the same class with Gregory. However we now give up that objection with this proviso that you will be more studious than you have been hitherto and that your hours of school or of study will not be neglected by your taking lessons on the Flute. When do you intend to learn fencing.

I am much amazed that you should be *tricked* out of your newspapers. I shall speak to Mr Barrett on the subject and give directions to have the paper in future directed to Mr Shine. Do not my dear child believe any of the foolish reports you may hear about your Father. Even were he found guilty they can only confine him a short time or fine him. Before I send off this letter tomorrow I shall be able to tell you if the trial will be put off until after Easter. Should it be put off as your Father expects it will, he purposes please God leaving here tomorrow for Liverpool on his way to London accompanied by James and F[*illegible*] who is becoming a great person *entirely*. Maurice will go over as soon as his petition against North comes on when I hope he will be the sitting Member for Drogheda.[14]

I suppose you know that Morgan has given up his Commission in the Austrian service. Your Father did not wish him to return to it. If the Union was repealed he hopes to get Morgan into the british service. John has entered the Kings Inns as a law student. He says he will be very industrious when he is called to the bar. It will be so sweet to be able to earn money for his *own use*. I hope he will keep his resolution.

Morgan John is come up. He left his brother Maurice at Exeter School in the county Carlow. Phrey Mynahan is away to leave his brother at the Carlow College. What fools they are not to leave their brothers at your College the only real good catholic school in Ireland.

Did you hear the Marquis of Anglessy was pelted with *Mud* the other day when riding through the streets. He is now as unpopular as he was popular before. I dont grudge that to him for his treatment to your dear Father. I wish my child you would if possible go to Communion on the 2[d] of February the purification and offer it up for the protection of your beloved Father from his Enemys. If you cant go on that day go on the next Sunday and offer up a Mass on the 2[d] for him and implore the intersession of the Virgin in his person as well as in your own.

Mr Nicholson we did not hear from since he left Dublin. Ellen, FitzSimon, sweet Mary and Christy are here since Wednesday. We had not room for *O Connell* and his sweet Mary is a sweet little Duck. She talks a great deal and when the day is wet she says slily to her Father *'Pip* (a pet name she has got for him) this is a fine day for the young *Ducks.'* I have not heard from Darrinane Abby since I last wrote. Bess Leyne has called her seventh son Daniel O Connell Leyne.

Did you get back the skates. When I sent to ask for them the clerk said he sent them here long since by one of the boys belonging to the chapel but they were not brought. You should get your Master to inquire for them.

Your Father is getting presents every day from the people. Orange scarfs orange and green Waistcoats. A snuff box with a picture of King William in it. A beautiful Irish diamond Harp with Irish Gold, an orange and green cloth cap and this day I got from the Jewellers two Medaelins gold with a figure in silver. Much of them representing your Father. They are very handsome.[15]

[*remainder missing*]

12. *Mary O'Connell to Daniel O'Connell Jr*

Monday Morning [31 January 1831]

My dear child

I write these few lines to tell you your Father leaves for Liverpool this day at 5 O Clock. We go down with him and start at one o clock as we shall be some time going down in consequence of the crowd of people who are to accompany him. Thank God he is quite well and in the best spirits in spite of his Enemys. Pray for him my dear child and take care of yourself and let me have the comfort to hear you are applying closely to your business. With fond love from your Father Sisters and Brothers. Believe me always

your fond Mother
Mary Ô Connell

My darling child this moment 10 O Clock your Father got a Notice from the court that he should appear tomorrow there under his recognizance and cannot go as he intended to day. They may keep him interned. He will however go down with us to Dunleary to gratify the trades who are to accompany him there with their banners. He will then speak to them.

13. *Mary O'Connell to Daniel O'Connell Jr*

Merrion Square
[February 1831]

My dearest Danny

I suppose the heavy fall of snow prevented the post from Clare and your post boy from travelling which has been the cause of my being so long without hearing from you. The fall of snow here and the hard frost which has followed will I trust be the means of giving you some skaiting. That is if your Skates have not been lost which I suspect has been the case. There are a few sledings here. The property of officers and of Mr Keogh the Barrister they look very pretty particularly at Night when they have boys with torchs before them. They pass by here shouting for your Father and the repeal of the Union.

After I wrote my letter to you last Monday we proceeded to Dunleary. Never did I witness such a scene any thing to equal the crowds and the enthusiasm I never witnessed. The trades with their different banners added much to the beauty of the procession. The day was beautiful and your Father looking so well and in such good spirits. When we got to the Pier he beged of the trades and the people to return as he would not go on board until he saw them all off. He did this to prevent them from knowing he was prevented by Government from leaving Ireland lest they may be exasperated. They obeyed his commands and arrived in Dublin without the least accident occurring to any person and we stopped to dine at the hotel there and in the evening returned to Dublin.

It is thought your Fathers trial will come on next Monday and that he will be found guilty though without cause. Should such be the case they can only confine him for a short time but I dont think they will be so foolish as to find him guilty. I put my trust in the great God who has hitherto protected him and will continue to do so. You shall hear the result of the trial. Mr Barrett promised John for me yesterday that he would send your paper by his own servant to the post office so as to insure its being sent from here. Let me know if you got it. Ellen and her babes are here still. Mary got a present to day from Letitia Costigan of two dressed *Dolls* one in Ladys dress the other in an officers dress. The moment she saw the officer she cried out that is my *Unty* Danny. The face nearly is like you. You see she does not forget you.

John dined yesterday for the first time at the Kings Inns. He dines there again to day.

You have seen Mr Nicholson so he mentions to Kate and I was glad to hear that Mr Esmond told him you were become more studious since your fathers visit than you were before. Continue that attention my dear Child and you will make your Father more fond of you and your Mother more happy. Just this moment a box arrived from Manchester containing a present to your Father of two China Jugs and an Irish stand beautifully ornamented with Gold Harps and Shamrocks. We have got addresses innumerable which you will have great pleasure in reading please God at Easter if you continue a good boy which I am very sure you will.

Kit Costigan talks of going to see Gregory very soon. All his family are quite well. Not a word of news in Dublin. I have this moment heard Julia had a letter from you yesterday. I am glad to hear from you in any way but you ought to write here once every week. I shall send this by the post this day if your Father is in time to give me a frank and should I have any news I shall mention it to you. I have just got a line from Maurice to say his Fathers trial is to take place on next tuesday week. His motion was

[*remainder missing*]

14. *Mary O'Connell to Daniel O'Connell Jr*

Friday Morning [February 1831]

My dearest Danny

Yesterdays post brought me the first letter I got from you for the last fortnight. I cannot however blame you for not writing when you were ill with a cold and particularly when your eyes appear to be affected. Do not my child use any cold applications with your eyes. Bathe them three times each day with water as hot as can bear it and do not read by candle light until they are quite well. This will be given to you by Mr O Connor to whom I write and to whom your newspaper shall in future be dirrected to insure your getting it in due time.

We are all thank God quite well escaped cold during the snow which was very severe in Dublin and its neighbourhood. Your dear Father is in good spirits notwithstanding the persecution of my Lord Anglessy who I assure you is at this moment very unpopular. Your Father's trial comes on next Thursday and with the assistance of God he will be triumphantly acquitted. I hope my dear child you continue to pray from him. You should every day until the trial is over. Offer up the sacrifice of the Mass for him and also your Communion either on next Sunday or on Sunday week if you have not been lately at Communion and ask Gregory to do the same. You shall hear from me immediately after the trial is over and all the circumstances attending it that I can send you.

Kit Costigin intends going to Clongows next week. I will send you the paper by the next opportunity and some fruit for Lent. Would you like some fruit Sandwiches or Jam Cakes as you used to call them. Say if you wish for any thing else. I beg my dear child you will write to me every week. I deserve this attention from you. I inclose this letter and Allys to Mr O Connor. Mr Nicholson will pay you another visit before he comes back. I cant get any account of his letter to you. Your Father mentioned it. No news in Dublin but what the papers will give you. James Con<nor> is not come to Dublin. Danny M< . . . > is going to Exeter. Your Uncle Finn and Phrey Mynahan are expected to Dublin next week. The latter *must* go see you. Your Father sisters and brothers unite in fond love to you with my dearest Danny your fond Mother

Mary O Connell

love to Gregory

15. *James O'Connor to Mary O'Connell*

My Dr Madam

I received your letter by this mornings post. I am happy to have it in my power to inform you that Danny is in the enjoyment of perfect good health. He had a little cold during the severe weather — but a little gentle medicine with care removed it very soon. His eyes were also a little inflamed but they have not the smallest appearance of inflammation at the present moment. He tells me that they become a little sore towards evenings but that it wears away again before <morning?>. The directions which you have <sent?> me about them shall be strictly adhered to. He promises me that he will <write?> to you punctually every week.

< . . . > all overjoyed to hear that you have so <litt>le apprehension for the result of Mr O'Connells trial. May God protect him against his enemies! We are all praying for him. Maurice will do me a great favour indeed by giving me the result of the trial by Thursdays post. We shall be all anxiety until we hear the result. May I beg you will present my kindest compliments to Mr O Connell & to my friends Maurice and Morgan I remain Dr Madam

> very sincerely
> Y^r Obd^t humble Servt
> J. O Connor

Clongowes Wood
Feby 12th 1831

16. *Mary O'Connell to Daniel O'Connell Jr*

> Merrion Square
> Monday the 21st [February 1831]

My darling Danny

I waited to hear from your Father on his arrival before I would write to you. This morning I had a second letter from him saying he was quite well and free from all fatigue after his unpleasant journey. He was nine hours going to the head all that time very sick. Got very bad posting up to London where he did not arrive until 10 O Clock on last Thursday Night. This night he is to contradict Mr Stanley in the house for the lying statement he gave to the government of your Fathers having entered into a compromise with the Attorney General respecting the prosecution. He will give it to all the good Folks as they deserve no charity from him. I hope you get the Pilot regularly.

Maurice is in Killkenny canvassing for the liberal candidate Colonel Butler who they hope will be returned. Maurice will next Month proceed to London about his own petition and will I trust sit in the house very shortly as Member for Drogheda. The Fitz Simons leave us on Wednesday. Poor little O'Connell has been very dangerously ill. He is now recovering. Mary is a great darling and Christy a sweet babe. The former is always speaking of *Unty Danny*.

Did you get the prog and the writing paper I sent you. Have you leave for Lent. We have the same as usual. Poor Mr Nicholson is too ill at Mr Farrells to come to Dublin. He is however out of danger. You will be sorry to hear poor Mr Teahan is dead. He died this day week was ill for some days. He was buried in the Abbey. When the good news of your Father arrived in Cahirsivine the town was illuminated and the country in a *blaze* with lampires. It is said that Honoria Primrose is to be married to Mr Pat Trant and Ellen McSwiny to Maurice Brennan. She denies it all in her letter to Betsy. Boris [?] is quite well and a great pet to your Aunt and to Ellen. Phrey Mynahan will call to see you on his way home the close of this week. No news in Dublin. I may soon have some news for you.

Are your eyes quite well. Dont use anything but hot water. Eye water of any kind is not at all servicable to the eye. I hope my child you are attending to your studies. Recollect that in six weeks from yesterday will be Easter Sunday. I sent off your letter to Ally Franked by your Father. I hope you attend to the cleanliness of your head and of your person. Do not I beg of you neglect this of all things.

O Donoughue has just called. He came to Dublin on business and goes off tomorrow. He is grown very tall and thin and not as well looking as he was. All his family quite well. Mrs O Donoghue had the measles lately. She is living near Killarney. How is Gregory. *Pope* pius the 16th. Mary sends you a kiss. She hopes to see [you] *pease tod* [*please God*] next Easter. You will doat of her when you see her. She has so much prate [?] and is so merry. Stranger is in *good health*. Your Sisters and brothers unite in fond love to you with my dearest Danny

> your ever fond Mother
> Mary O'Connell

17. *Mary O'Connell to Daniel O'Connell Jr*

> Merrion Square
> Wednesday [23 February 1831]

My dearest Danny

I am very much amazed that you do not write to me regularly every week. Your last letter I got on Monday and the letter before on last Friday week. I have sent you the paper and the pencils you wished for and the money I will send by Kit Costigin who speaks of going down to Clongows the latter end of this week. I will only send you a few shillings for if you deserve to be brought up at Easter they will be sufficient for all your expences notwithstanding the *closeness* and *scarcity* of the times. I will also send you a drawing of *Strangy* taken from life by your brother John. You will consider it a good likeness. Perhaps Gregory could make *interest* with him to send him a drawing of *his* dog Fan.

I hear from your Father every day. His business came on in the house on Monday last but until tomorrow we cant hear the result of it. As far as it went on that night it was favourable to the Man of the people. Maurice is not yet returned from Kilkenny. He will leave tomorrow or next day for London as his petition [against North's election in Drogheda] is to come on the 7th of March. Your Father hopes he will be the sitting Member for Drogheda. Great fears are entertained that O Gorman Mahon will lose his seat now that he has taken the honest side. I should regret his losing his seat.

Dublin is as stupid as possible. We dont of course go to the Theatre in Lent and the Girls would not go to Lord Anglessys drawing room for his conduct to your Father. My next letter will perhaps contain more news you will be glad to hear. You must not speak of it even to Gregory and burn this letter as well as the letter that will contain this *news*.

We heard from Ellen today. She and her babes are quite well. I heard yesterday from your Mama B. She desires her fondest love to you. No news from Kerry lately. Boris [?] is very well. Phrey was obliged to leave Dublin without going to see you. He will come up at Easter when I hope you will see him here. John did not go in for the last examination. He is very idle. I hope you will never be so idle. He is become a Member of the Kings Inns as a preparation to become a Barrister. Morgan I suppose you know has left the Austrian service.

We are all well but very lonely. Little Mr Nicholson is still at Ballina. He was very ill and still unable to write. Mr L'Estrange will be home next summer. He has been very ill. Mr Whelan always inquires for you as indeed all your friends do.

Report says Pat Trant is to be married to Honoria Primrose and Ellen McSwiny to Maurice Brennan. Ellen denies this charge most lustily [?]. Mary would not marry Doctor Barry. Dont mention this.

On second thoughts I send you by the Clongows Car a canister containing ten shillings and some peppermint Lozenges. Do you eat meat every day but Wednesday Friday and Saturday. Are you quite well. Your Sisters and brothers unite in fond love to you with my dearest Danny

your fond Mother
Mary Ô Connell

18. *Mary O'Connell to Daniel O'Connell Jr*

Merrion Square
Tuesday Evening
March the 8th 1831

private

My dearest Danny

The *secret* I spoke of was not the intended marriage of Miss Costigan which is now too public to be a secret any longer. What would you think of the possibility of a *wedding* taking place at 30 Merrion Square South. On this subject you must be very discreet as on this side of the grave there is no certainty but that of death. Should you speak of what I am going to tell you to Gregory you must first get his *honour* he will not mention it to any person until you get leave from me which shall be as soon as I think there may be a wedding. At present it is uncertain.

Now to the secret. What do you think of Betseys having made a conquest of a Mr Ffrench a Catholic young Gentleman of good fortune of Ffrench Lawn in the County Roscommon. He is not handsome but a fine made large Man with a very good countenance and a great favourite to all who know him. He bears a most amiable character and *we* all like him greatly *including Betsey*. His Father is but a short time dead. He has no brother two sisters one married the other single. His Mother lives at present at Ffrench Lawn. You are aware that the Ffrenchs are all highly respectable and our friend is the descendant of one of the oldest catholic familys of the name in Connaught. All I have to say farther that such a thing as a marriage may occur but when I cannot well tell you.

You were sorry I dare say to hear Maurice did not succeed in his petition against North. Perhaps it is all for the better. Your Father is quite well. His address is 16 Manchester Buildings. Westminster. He will I hope be home at Easter. Poor little Christy FitzSimon was near dying last Thursday of Convulsions. He is now quite out of danger and Mary and O Connell are quite well and merry.

Our friends in Kerry we seldom hear from. We have got at Darrinane parish in poor Mr Teahans place the Revd *Patrick* O'Connell. I am told a very clever Man. Mr Nicholson is still at Ballina. He will call to see you before he comes back. Dont upset me. The time is now so short when I hope to have the happiness to see you here.

Did I tell you that poor Keane late of the Theatre here died suddenly. His son has got the situation his Father held and Calcraft is to give the Widow a clear benefit at the Theatre.

I have no more news to tell you. Dublin is so stupid. It was very stupid of me to forget sending you Strangers picture. The next opportunity I shall send it. You did not answer my question. If you have leave to eat meat this Lent. Do you get the Pilot more regularly than you did before your Father went to London. I shant send this letter until tomorrow as I expect to see Edward Coffy to be able to tell you if he is to go to Edinburgh with Sir Edward Lies who is ordered there in the same situation he held here in the post office.

Wednesday morning. I heard this post from your Father. He is quite well. Edward Coffy was here yesterday morning. He is now in the dead letter office and if he does not get a better situation Sir Edward Lies is to take him to Scotland with him next month. Poor felow was very ill in a fever last December. He is grown tall and wears a *wig*. With love from your sisters and brothers. Believe me my dear child

always your fond Mother
Mary Ô Connell

19. *Mary O'Connell to Daniel O'Connell Jr*

Merrion Square
Saturday [19 March 1831]

My dearest Danny

I was delighted to hear from Christopher Costigin that you are quite well and happy. The notice he gave me was so short I had not time to write or to send you any prog. Money I am sure you will not want until you come up at Easter. Pray tell me in your next on what day you all go to your Easter duty that I may make arrangements to have you here on Easter Saturday please God. Dan O Sullivan will probably go down for you. What place have you got in your class. Have you got a premium in Arithmatick. You were always clever at 'making figures as the country Man said of his son'.

I got your letter last Thursday but it was by post it came here. Who was the Gentleman Gregory and you were going to fish with yesterday. You are so witty. I expect you were. '*He* was a queer fishing *rod* for us to make use of.' What did Christopher say to Gregory about accompanying you to Town at Easter *tide*.

You will be surprised to hear that your cousin Ricarda has got a young daughter. Last Sunday I had a letter from John Primrose ment-ing [*mentioning*] it. She was confined at Killgrave and attended by your friend Doctor Barry. Both she and the child were quite well. I wish it was a son. There are so many females in the family at present. Ellen Connor [cousin] is at Killgrave. The Baby will I suppose be called Betsy.

John Primrose mentions your Boat brought in a piece of timber worth five pound she found at Sea part of an unfortunate wreck. You will be very proud of your *vessel*. Ally is quite well. She has the new Parish Priest with her until his own home is ready. His name is O Connell. Jack is very well taken care of.

You will be glad to hear Maurice is gone down this *morning* to be *returned* for Clare. The Mahons resigned as the people would not return either of them free of expense though they were to do so by Maurice. Charles O Connell came up last Night for Maurice. The Gentry and the people sent for him. They would not hear of any other candidate. It is thought there will be no contest. The feeling is all favour of Maurice. Sir Edward O Brien is the other Candidate. It is thought he will give up as he has succeeded in turning out the Mahons. Maurice is tomorrow to be met twelve miles from Ennis by all the trades with banners accompanied by the people and a great number of the Gentry. Maurice is then to enter. I hope as the conquering [King of?] Ennis. Wont you be very proud of having your brother an M.P. as well as your Father from whom I heard this morning. He hopes to be here the close of the last week of Lent.

Betsy will probably change her name before next Month is at an end. This between you and me. Mr Ffrench is very anxious to see you. He is very amiable and I am sure you will like him as much as we all do.

Ellen and her darlings are all well. She Fitz and Mary will be in Town in time for the *approaching* event in this family. Your Grand Mother is quite well. I have written to beg she would come up to see all her children here. The Girls, Morgan, and John unite in fond love to you with my dearest Danny

your ever affectionate
Mother.
Mary O Connell

Hannah and Julia desire their love and Dog Stranger his *respects*.

20. *Mary O'Connell to Daniel O'Connell Jr*

Merrion Square
Wednesday [23 March 1831]

My dearest Danny

I got your letter this morning and in reply can only say a few words. If you came up from school before Easter Sunday you would not have any time to stop here after Easter week. Therefore Kit Costigan will be with you by twelve o clock on Easter Sunday and you will be here please God to dinner on that day. For many reasons it is better not to ask leave for you to come sooner as I should be refused or else your time would be limited for return on *low* Monday.

I heard this day from your Father and Maurice. They are both well. I hope the next time I should write to you I shall have to tell you Maurice is Member for Clare. All his friends *there* are of his being returned.

Mr Ffrench was introduced to us by Maurice. He dined here last December and the first day he saw Betsy he was *capti*vated. He is of a high [?] catholic family. Of his appearance you must judge for yourself. He is truly amiable and good. Betsy is getting a very handsome carriage built at Kutters. Chocolate colour. *He* is about [to] buy handsome bay horses. And the Ffrench livery is blue and yellow. The same as Lord Anglessys. This is all the information I can give you at present. FitzSimon came here last evening. He left Ellen and the babes quite well. Mary when any thing is done to vex her lays her little head on the sopha and says 'Im angry now.'

I hope my darling boy you will make a worthy communion on Easter Sunday. Pray for all of us but in particular for your Brothers that they may become religious. When you are coming up borrow the clouths as you say or send me your measure taken by *your* Tayler and I shall have a new suit of clouthes ready for Easter Sunday. I have no news. We are all very well but very busy preparing for a certain event. With love from your Sisters and brothers believe me my dearest Danny Ever your fond Mother

Mary Ô Connell

love from all here to Gregory the 16 and the most pious

21. *Catherine (Kate) O'Connell to Daniel O'Connell Jr*

Merrion Square
March 25th 1831

My dear Danny

I set down in a great hurry to let you know that Mama received Maurice's first frank. Sir Edward O Brien gave up at three o clock on Tuesday. Indeed he was beaten as Maurice was a hundred & sixty a head.

My Father is also in great spirits as the second reading of the reform Bill was carried by a majority of *one*.

All your friends here are quite well. Mama would write to you yourself but she has to write to the new M.P.

Mama wishes to know if you will send her yr. measure for clothes as the sooner you do so the better. I am in a great hurry which must excuse this short letter.

Stranger desires his best regards to you & Greg. Betsey and her *Caro* [Nicholas Ffrench] are just gone out to walk in the Square. Stranger always goes with them & to tell the truth I believe *he* would wish to have *lovers* always to walk with. They stay out so long.

Mr. L Estrange is to be home very soon now. Poor Mr Nicholson has been very ill since. He will soon be coming to town & if he is able is to pay you a visit.

Greg must hear all the Dublin news as Anne wrote to him yesterday.

All unite in love with dear Dan

your fondly affectionate
Sister Kate Ô Connell

22. *Mary O'Connell to Daniel O'Connell Jr*

[28 March 1831]

My dear Danny

In reply to your letter in which Betsey got this morning I send you the inclosed for Mr O Connor. Lose no time sending your Measure as in all probability you will want the Clouths to be ready before you. The

Carriage shall be at Clongows by Nine O Clock on Sunday Morning next please God for you and Gregory, and I believe Mr O Connor should he wish to come to Dublin. If he does not come in the carriage with you both you can give a seat to some other person if you wish.

You will perceive by the Frank that Maurice is come home. Take care of the Frank as it is his first to you. He is quite well and merry. I heard to day from your Father. He hopes to be here on Saturday next.

All our friends in Wicklow are quite well. I write in a great hurry so must conclude. With love from your Sisters and Brothers. Believe me my dear Danny

Ever your fond Mother
Mary O Connell

P S The Clouths you are now to get must answer you for the Summer Vacation please God. Christopher Costigin cant go for you. It is no matter.

23. *Mary O'Connell to Daniel O'Connell Jr*

private

Dont you or Gregory tell any of the Boys or any other person how long you are to stay here. Should they ask you say 'some days'.

Merrion Square
Friday April the 1st 1831

My dearest Danny

You will not be sorry to hear your Father arrived here this morning soon after seven o clock. He had only five hours passage by the Head. He is thank God quite well but looks thin which I attribute to his strict fasting during the Lent. He desires his fond love to you but *fears* you may have *some objection* to *coming up* on Sunday. Pray why dont you tell me of your places in the school. I hear you have got the first in every thing.

I got a letter yesterday from Mr Connor giving you leave for a *week* to which I will add another week. He will let you and Gregory start early as possible on Sunday next. The Carriage shall arrive at Clongows by Nine O Clock. You must take care the Driver hears Mass in your Chapel and that he gets his breakfast before you leave. You can be here with ease at four o clock should you leave Clongows at one o clock. Dont let the Driver stop any where either to feed his horses or to drink. They will be all fresh enough stopping from the time they get to Clongows until you leave it.

I got your Measure this morning from Maurice. Your clouths shall if possible be ready for Sunday. Tell Gregory I sent to his Mama to write at once for leave for him to come up from Mr Connor. I am sure she wrote before to him on that subject. In great haste believe me your fond Mother

Mary Ô Connell

24. *Mary O'Connell to Daniel O'Connell Jr*

London April the 23ᵈ 1831

My dearest Danny

I have been in vain expecting a letter from you this week. I was glad to hear from John you had returned to school last Monday and that your Cold was quite gone with the exception of a slight remains of your Cough which I trust is now compleatly gone. You should attend to the directions given you by the Doctor and above all things to take care not to get wet in your feet. You must please God bathe this vacation every day to lay in a store of health. I beg you will write to me once every week.

This letter your Father takes to Ireland for which place he leaves London on Monday next to be reelected for Waterford and Maurice I hope for Clare.

We saw the King pass to the house yesterday to [*illegible word*] the parliament which is dissolved this day. He was greatly cheered, but except the beauty of his horses *our* own grand procession to Kingstown [Dún Laoghaire] was much better worth seeing and infinitely superior.

We stop here until your Father and Maurice return to us after the Elections are over and we shall all please God be over in July. Your Father will probably pay you a visit so will Maurice. Did you read his

Murder speech [unidentified]. Every body was delighted with him, particularly his Father who says Maurice has *more* talent than his Father. I shall be quite satisfied if Maurice has half as much talent as his Father has.

We shall be very lonely after them. I wish the parliament had dissolved during the last week of Lent. We should not be hurried here as we were. In this life we cannot have every thing as we wish.

We heard to day from Ellen. All well there. Betsy stops for another week with Ellen.

Did you think of speaking to James about the Gunn. I hope my dear child you will deserve this present from your Mod.

You did not tell me if you dined with Costello the day you were at Dunleary with us. I have no news to tell you. London is not very gay. I wish from my heart the Union was repealed when we could stay at home. All our friends in Kerry are quite well. Report says Mary Anne O Connell is to be married to an officer. Son to Mr White of Glengarr. I dont believe a word of it.

Sunday night. I have nothing further to tell you. Your Father and Maurice start tomorrow. I saw Kit Costigin this day in the street walking with John. Direct you[r] letters to 5 Parliament Street Westminster. We change to that number tomorrow a change much for the better. Good Night my dear Child and believe me always your fond Mother M O Connell

Mr Nicholson is still in the country. He is better. Mr L'Estrange will be home this summer. Kate got a letter from *him* the day after we got to London. Is your cough well.

25. *Mary O'Connell to Daniel O'Connell Jr*

Monday [May] the 9th 1831

My darling Danny

I got your letter from Clongows on Wednesday after much anxiety at your long silence. The Cough you complained of is I trust by this time quite gone but this bitter weather you must be very cautious of cold and not overheat yourself by exercising too much. You need not put on long stockings until the Winter sets in.

We are quite well here but very lonely after your Father and Maurice. I heard this morning from the former who is by this time in Tralee. He was to have a public entrance last evening to that Town. The trades were all to meet him accompanied by the people and in spite of my Lord Kenmares opposition will be the Member for Kerry probably before this day week.

Maurice is also sure of success in Clare. It is also thought that O Gorman Mahon will be returned for Clare. The *Terry Alts* say he must go out. This I regret as I like him better than Mahon.

Kate had a letter to day from Ellen. She and her babes are quite well. FitzSimon is down at Clare with Maurice. Betsy and Ffrench leave Dublin on Wednesday next for Ffrench Lawn. After their County Election they will go on a tour of pleasure to the Giants causeway. John will not I believe go with them. He is not quite recovered from his cold. Hanna will see you before this reaches you. Also Julia. Mr Esmond called to see me the other day. He is going away this week. I also saw Kenny [?] Russell who is become an uncommon nice young Man. I saw *all* the Men Costigins here. Kit is gone to Paris. Kate will write on the other side of this letter and give you all the news. I hope to get a frank from Shiel who is again returned for a borough. He is here with his Wife and family. Good by my dearest Danny. Believe me ever

your fond Mother
Mary Ô Connell

[*Kate O'Connell adds approximately 250 words describing a theatrical she attended*]

26. *Mary O'Connell to Daniel O'Connell Jr*

[London]
[12 May 1831]

My dear child

I had a letter to day from your Father from Ennis where he was enthusiasticly received by the trades of the Town and the people who went out some Miles to meet him. He was also received in the same way at Limerick and yesterday was to have a grand entrance to Tralee. His return for Kerry is quite certain. Also dear Maurices return for Clare. He will be at the head of the poll. I dont yet know if Mahon will be the other Member. I have no more news. I think this letter will be welcome to you. I inclose it under care of a frank to Hanna. Ever my dear Child.

Believe me your fond Mother
Mary Ô Connell
Tuesday

27. *Mary O'Connell to Daniel O'Connell Jr*

London, June the 7th [1831]

Why my dearest Danny do you write to every person save and except your poor Mod who has suffered so much uneasiness and agony of mind for the last 5 weeks.

All is now thank God happily over and our dear Maurice has not the serious sin to answer for of having fought a duel. Of course you have seen all the details in the Pilot therefore it is unnecessary to say any more on this to me very painful subject. I suspect your dear Father and dear Maurice on Saturday next. They will arrive from Ennis tomorrow in Dublin and leave it the next day for Liverpool. I shall send this letter under care to your Father.

I cannot tell you for some days after your Fathers arrival what time it may be likely we shall leave for Ireland. I hear the Session will last a great while. What would you think of passing your Vacation with us here. I hope we may be over by the end of July. When I am certain the exact time I shall be in Ireland I will at once write to Mrs Costigan and persecute her with letters until she promises to let dear Gregory come with you to the Abby.

Ellen and her babes are still in Dublin. I suppose you have heard that *Julia* is in a fair way to give an heir to the name of O Brien. John talks of going to spend some weeks at Ffrench Lawn. Betsy will stop there until she comes to the Abby. She is very gay going to dinner partys and to Races. She is going to stop a week at Doo Castle the seat of a Mr

McDamea [?] a Cousin of Ffrench. Kate had a letter today from Ellen McSwiny. She was at the Christening of young O Donaghue. It was grand and stupid. *He* is named Daniel after his great Grand father and his Fathers brother. The Sponsors were Morgan John and Miss O Donaghue. Mrs O Donaghue is in very delicate health but her baby is a fine healthy child. Strangy and Boris [?] are quite well. They know your Father and Maurice quite well. The Mynahans are living in Killarney. James Connor is at present in Dublin attending the term. Ricardas little daughter is I am told very pretty.

Kate will soon write you a great deal of amusing intelligence. She is a better correspondent than I am. She is fond of writing and I hate it. Answer this without delay and direct under cover to Maurice '5 Parliament Street London'. You have no notion what a fine English accent Thomas had when he left this. I hope his sojourn in Kerry has not spoiled it. I am happy to tell you Ally is [to] be Mistress of Darrinane at this present moment and she h[as] hitherto acted with the strictest justice by me and by those under her command. Moore I am to pardon on condition that he makes an ample apology to Ally. Jack darling is quite well and the *Abby* looking beautiful. I wish we could be all there the 3ᵈ of August.

How is Mr Nicholson. Mr L'Estrange is in Paris on his way home. Give my love to Gregory. Kate and Morgan unite in fond love to you with my darling Danny your fond Mother

Mary Ô Connell

28. *Mary O'Connell to Daniel O'Connell Jr*

London June the 26ᵗʰ 1831

My dearest Danny

I had the honour of getting your letter (begun this day week) on Thursday last. I suppose the cold you had was the influenza which is quite rife here. Thank God I have as yet escaped. Your Father, Kate and Morgan had it Maurice slightly and the three servant Men and Kates Maid also took it. You may judge what a house full of Invalids we had.

Thank God they are all now quite well. John mentioned he James Connor and Hanna had the prevailing cold. John is by this time at Ffrench Lawn.

I am anxious to know if the pain in your side is quite gone and if you are free from all Cough. Be particular in telling me all about your health. Are you preparing to get a premium.

I am about buying you a detonating Gun which Maurice seems to approve of. The only objection I have to buy it is that I should prefer getting one in Ireland for you. The English have enough of money without getting any from us. That we can give to our own poor Country.

We are all heartily sick of London but hope to be out of it by the last week in July. We purpose going from Milford haven to Waterford where I fancy you would have no objection to join us. You may depend upon my getting leave for Gregory to go with you this Vacation to the Abbey.

Kit Costigin is here on his way home from Paris. Surgeon Carbut [?] is afraid Gregorys fingers will always remain contracted. For God sake take care and dont meet with any accident and dont overheat yourselve by too much exercise. You will soon have a visit of a day from a very dear friend of yours can you guess who I mean and will you promise to be glad to see *him*. He talks of leaving London the close of this week. I fancy I hear you say 'ah Mod who is he' as you are so *curious* I shall write his name. 'Frances Joseph L'Estrange' I am happy to tell you he is looking very well. He only arrived on Friday last. He was quite a surprise upon us.

John Sheil was here to day. I did not see him. His Mother and sister are to be here tomorrow. Were you not very glad to see your Father. Do you ever write to Betsey. No news from Kerry. Your Mama B was ill but is now quite well. We shall go to the Abbey by Tralee to spend some days there to see her. They talk of having a Regatta there this summer. There are to be no races in Killarney this year but Maurice is to have Races near Carhen instead of having them at Ballinskelligs quite independent of the *tide*. We must *all* go there. Maurice says Jack is as fat and as saucey as you please. The Water Guards have been taken from our station and sent to Waterville. Mick Kelly is quite well.

Monday Morning. We had letters to day from Ellen Betsey and John. They are all quite well but no news of any kind. We dined yesterday with Mr and Mrs Phillips. They have a nice family of two daughters and one very fine Boy. All the Irish Members are in Town. I wish they were obliged to leave London before the close of this month. I fear we shant be off from here until the first week in August. The reform bill will I trust pass before then.

This letter is very stupid but Kate will next week write you a long and an amusing letter. Mr Nicholson is in the County Galway. He is much better. Give the inclosed at once. It is from young Kelly. With love from your Father Kate Maurice Morgan and from Mr L'Estrange who is just here. Believe me my dear child ever your fond Mother

Mary Ô Connell

29. *Mary O'Connell to Daniel O'Connell Jr*

[London]
[9 July 1831]

My dearest Danny

I suppose your silence is occasioned by your examinations therefore I shall not complain. My last letter remains still unanswered as the last one I got from you was only in return for a previous letter of mine. I have had the happiness to hear of you through Mrs Costigin. The account she gives of your appearance and of the state of your health is truly gratifying to me. She also spoke of your having every chance of a premium this examination. I fondly hope it will be the case and that Mondays post will bring me a statment to that effect from yourself.

Dear Gregory. What a severe accident he met with. I am happy to hear there is every prospect of his recovering the use of his fingers. Mrs Costigin has not yet promised me to let *him* go to the Abbey however I hope to prevail upon her to do so. I much fear parliament will not be over before the 1st of September. You did not answer me the question I asked you namely how you would like to spend one Month of your vacation in London should we be detained here. We have an idea of hav-

ing you come over in the Steam packet to London that is if any friend
of ours happened to be coming over. How does Edward Russell intend
to travel. He is I know to spend this vacation in England. Ask him and
let me know exactly what he says and your wish as to coming here in
preference to going to Ballenamena to wait our arrival in Ireland.

Mr L'Estrange is still here. He talks of going to Morrow Night in the
Mail for Liverpool. He is looking well and will shortly pay you a visit.
To him I refer you for an account of Windsor Palace. He accompanied
us there last Sunday. It is a splendid thing. Mr Nicholson is in the
County Galway much improved in his health.

The Shiels are here. They came over to see Hugh William. They are
gone to day with Kate and Morgan to see the Town. We are all quite
sick of London but you would be delighted with it. There are so many
sights. John is at Ffrench Lawn and will stop there until he accompanys
Betsy and Ffrench to the Abby. Poor James Connor has been very ill
with an inflamation of the chest at the Square. He is not yet able to
travel. His brother Maurice has passed his examinations at Edingbor-
ough with great success. He returns to Tralee an M.D. immediately.

Report says Ellen McSwiny is to be married to Kade [?] Murphy. She
denys it but I dont mind that. Alicia Mynahan has refused Maurice Brennan!!! and Miss O Donoghue is to be married immediately to Mr Jerry
Stack [?] Murphy son to Jerry Murphy of Cork the very rich Man brother
to the Bishop. Young O Donoghue is a fine stout Boy. Ricarda Primrose
has got a baby little girl. She is nursing her. No news from Kerry only
what you read in the paper. What do you think of your Cousin Dan. Your
Mama B has been very ill. She is now quite well and never forgets you.
She is very proud of having your Father Member for Kerry.

Your Father is thank God quite well though he and Maurice were
not in bed until three this Morning. They expect to have a Majority of
41 in the Lords in favour of the bill. Should the parliament sit late this
time they will not again meet until after Christmas. That is not until
February. You will be glad to hear Ally is now quite happy at the Abbey.
The Quirks are gone and *she* and old John O Connell agree very well.
Fogerty was down there making some necessary improvements. Marty

is there but in very bad health. Your *horse* is quite well. So is Boris [?]. You did not answer me about the Gun.

I suppose you know that Julia O'Brien is in a fine way of giving an heir to the *house* of *Thomend*. What a *curiosity* it will be. Your Aunt Mynahan is living in Killarney. I suppose you heard there is to be a Regatta in Tralee this summer and no Races in Killarney. Great doings are expected in Tralee. I hope we shall all be there together in preference to being here broiling. The heat is quite dreadful however we are in excellent health.

We dine to day with the Celebrated Barry O Mara[16] in company with Murrot's [*Murat's*] son and his Wife and I believe Madame Wise. We are to see all the present given by Napoleon to Barry O Mara. When next you write to Hanna or Julia tell them to send word to Mr Barret not to send you the Pilot after the 29th of the Month to stop it *entirely* until further orders. God bless you my dear dear Danny. Your Father, Kate and your brothers unite in fond love to you with your ever affectionate and attached *Mod*

Mary Ô Connell

love to Greg from *all* here

Mr L'Estrange is just here. He does not leave until Monday or Tuesday next. He desires his love to you and to Gregory. Charles O Connor has got a parish at Kidderminster. He likes England very much. The new chapel is *being* built at Darrinane.

Write to me at once and answer me all the questions I have asked you particularly respecting your vacation and the Gun. How is Mr Esmond and Mr O Connor. I hope you dont exercise too much <in?> This dreadful hot weather. Direct under cover to Maurice.

30. *Mary O'Connell to Daniel O'Connell Jr*

[9 November 1831]

My darling Danny

I have this moment seen your friend Hearn. He gives me a great account of your journey and of the pleasant time he spent at school with you. He says he left you in good health and spirits which I trust will continue now that the cholera is not realy in England. All the papers of the two last days contradict it from the best authority. Your Father is no longer afraid.

We heard to day from dear Maurice. Poor Phil Primrose's body has [not] yet been found and I fear it will not. God help his unhappy family. Maurice will stop there until all chance of finding the body is over and should it be found he will wait until after the interment.

I have no news for you at present. I shall write to you when I get your letter. We are all well. Let me know if you want any thing. Young Dewit was called to the bar on Monday and will be married immediately. Dan OSullivan came to Town yesterday. Mary FitzSimon desires her love to Uncle Danny and to Gregory. James Connor desires to tell you with his love he will soon go to see you.

I hope my darling Danny you will [pay] close attention to your studys. You owe it to yourself as well as to your Parents for the indulgence of the long vacation you had. Be attentive and make good use of the time you will be at Clongows. You have talents if you only give your mind to application. I am sure you will do every thing to gratify me.

With fond love from your Father, the Girls and John. I will now conclude. Ffrench and Morgan have not yet returned. Remember me to Gregory and believe me my darling Danny ever your truly

fond Mother
Mary Ô Connell

Wednesday

31. *Daniel O'Connell Jr to Mary O'Connell* (*in Dublin*)

Clongowes November 10th [1831]

My Dearest Mother

I received your letter yestoday and answer it that it may be time for the post. As Hearn has seen you I need give you no account of our journey all I say is we had great fun. Mr Curtis who knew Hearn before invited him down in the fine weather. I am obliged to you for the good store with which you filled my basket. If James Conner came down at Xmass or before it I will be very glad to see him. I mean 'Please God' to settle my tools in my table in straps when my store of cakes &c is out instead of keeping them in the small box as it will be more convenient. Tell Julia I will write to her soon 'Please God'. I did not speak about John's books yet. If I get them I will send them in the basket next Wednesday 'Please God'. I hope you'll answer this at once. Give my love to my Father, the girls, John, Julia, Hannah, James and Stranger whom I hope gets long walks every day. I am ever your very affectionate son

Daniel Ô Connell

263 days of *Vacation. Bad news!*

32. *Mary O'Connell to Daniel O'Connell Jr*

November the 12th 1831

My dearest Danny —

I write to day merely to say how much I feel your unkindness in not keeping your promise of writing to me. Had you not voluntarily promised to write to me on Sunday last I should not so much mind your letting nearly a week elapse without a single line. If illness prevented you from writing I am quite sure Mr O Conner would have the kindness to let me know of it. I fear it is your usual fault of putting off until tomorrow what you should do to day that has given me cause to complain of your silence. If you have not written before this reaches you may I beg you will prevail upon yourself to spare ten minutes to write to your Mother who will always feel pleasure when reading your letters as I am quite sure they will never cause me to experience the contrary towards you.

I hope you get the Pilot regularly. There is no news but the election of your friend John Finely to the Chairmanship of the County Galway.

I did not hear from Maurice these two days. Poor Phil Primroses body was not found last Wednesday. His family are in the deepest affliction. Had the poor fellow taken Maurices advice he would not have met a watery grave. The day fixed for the Regatta which by the by would have taken place if Maurice had been here or in London. Maurice refused to assist at it as the day was unfavourable, recommending to all those who were in boats to go home. Poor Phil agreed with Trant to have a boat race. Andy Creegh who was with Maurice got on board of Phils boat, but Maurice would not allow him to remain he being under his command. Thus was poor Andy, by his obedience saved from sharing poor Phils fate. I trust in God my dear Maurice will disperse of his yacht and keep to his good resolutions.

Ffrench and Morgan are not yet returned. Morgan is quite delighted with the hunting. The FitzSimons are home still. Mary is by me and desires her love to Uncle Danny. She is a sweet little baby.

I saw Mr Fitzpatrick[17] to day. He told me the brewery was to commence on next Monday. He also mentioned that all the [spirit] Grocers had entered into resolutions of becoming Publicans and determined only to take *your* Porter and Brew. With love from your Father and all your other friends here. I will now conclude with for this time forgiving you for not keeping your promise my dear child of writing to your fond

Mother Mary Ô Connell

33. *Mary O'Connell to Daniel O'Connell Jr*

November the 14th 1831

My dearest Danny

On your Fathers return from court last Saturday he gave me your letter which he got in there from a Mr Baineare [?]. I also got your letter this morning and now thank you for each of them.

I am delighted to find you were at Communion yesterday. I hope you offered it up for our dear Maurice who is not returned. Kate had a letter this morning from [him] written last Thursday. He is quite well but occupied looking for the body of poor [Phil] Primrose without any avail. If they did not get it on Friday their hopes of ever finding it should be given up. The poor afflicted family are in the deepest misery at this prospect which makes the dear fellows loss to them doubly melancholy. May the great God comfort them.

Betsy had a letter from Ffrench this morning. He mentions that Morgan and he are to go to Fort William to day to stop there until Monday next. They will be home on Tuesday week. I fear Maurice wont be home until the close of this week. John Primrose is unable to do your Father's business.[18] It therefore falls on Maurice to do it.

John bids me tell you with his love he is much obliged to you about the premiums. He wrote Dewits marriage settlements on Saturday evening under his Father's directions in the study. They will this day be ingressed [?] and probably by Thursday next the wedding will take place. Mr Dewit bought a splendid wedding present of Gold ornaments and a Watch and Chain for Alicia amounting in all to sixty five guineas.

I have no news to tell you. The Costigins are quite well. John had a letter from Kit on Saturday from Paris. He had been very ill but is now recovering fast. He writes from Paris. Sylvester is with him. Kit is to spend the Winter in Italy which will reestablish his health.

Mary is by me while I write. She desires her love to Uncle Danny and to tell him she is very good. When I got your letter this morning she was in a little bold fit and I read from your letter your love for to her and that you hoped she was a good girl. This had the best effect. She at once became quite good. She is a sweet baby.

Your Father has so many demands for fr<anks> I fear it impossible to get one. If I waited until tomorrow he would frank this letter but I thought you would prefer getting it tomorrow instead of Wednesday.

Should the Cholera come to Ireland we shall certainly go to the Abbey. Prayers against the contagion were yesterday offered up at all the Catholic Churches.

I think Mr Nicholson is a little jealous with you for not going to see him before you went to Clongows. Bessy O Connell told him her *story* last Saturday. She was yesterday at Communion. Were you realy pleased with the prog that was in the bottom of the basket for your use and Gregorys. Your Father Sisters Bessy and James Connor write in love to you my dear child with your ever fond Mother

Mary Ô Connell

Julia is a good deal better.
Stranger is quite well.

34. *Mary O'Connell to Daniel O'Connell Jr*

November the 24th 1831

My dearest Danny

I got the basket and the *notes* in closed last Night late by the CarMan as he leaves early to day for Clongows. I could not have the prog ready sooner than this evening and as tomorrow and the next day will be days of abstinence I think it will be better for you to get the basket on Sunday next by your cousin Morgan John who is going with some friends of his to visit the Jesuits. I shall send you a roast *Roscommon* Turkey some cold ham bread and a bottle of Rasberry Vinegar. I sent the Note to Mrs Costigan. I am sure she will send the Jam and some fruit in the basket. I shall also send the candles which Hanna forgot to send the last time and your pencils and peppermint you forgot.

Ffrench and Morgan arrived last night. They are quite well. Morgan quite delighted with Roscommon. Fort William he says is a very sweet place and Ffrench greatly beloved by all. Morgan is become thin and it becomes him also. Maurice is not yet arrived. He is busy with the tenantry. John Primrose cant attend to any business. Poor Phils body has not been found.

The parliament is to meet on the 6th of this Month. Your Father says he will not go until after Christmas if he can possibly avoid it which I trust may be the case.

Alicia was married on Tuesday. Her Marriage is given in the Limerick paper of yesterday as follows. 'Married yesterday by the Catholic Bishop of Kerry the right Revrd Doctor Eagan at her Mothers house in Killarney Thomas John Dewitt Esqr B[*illegible*] heir and son to our respected Citizen Thomas Dewitt to Alicia daughter of the late Phrey Mynahan Esqr of Rathbeg Co Kerry and Niece to Daniel OConnell M.P. Immediately after the ceremony the happy pair set off for New Park the seat of his Father in the Co Limerick.'

I have no news. The dinner to your Father last Sunday was most splendid. The Girls Mary Costigan and I went to listen to the speeching. The Committee gave me a room and plenty of Ice and Cakes. Also tea and [*illegible*]. Your Father spoke beautifully. You will see an account of all in the Pilot. My health was given with great eloquence and very well received.

Nothing can be more stupid than Dublin at this moment. There is no society not even with the Costigins. Mrs Norths house is to be sold. I hope we may get a good Neighbour in her place. Ellen and her *family* leave us on Saturday next. Mary often talks of *Untle* Danny. She is a sweet child a great darling to all of us. Tell Morgan John any thing you may wish to communicate secretly to me. I told him to take you out to walk with him without a third person. Your Father Sisters Brothers *Niece* and cousin Bessy desire their fond love to you with my dearest Danny

your ever fond Mother
Mary Ô Connell

I open this to tell you I send you the Kerry paper. It has some amusing extracts in it. Take *care* of it.

35. *Mary O'Connell to Daniel O'Connell Jr*

[November 1831]

My dear Danny

The inclosed letter to your Father yesterday I got franked and sent by the post to Ally who is at present quite happy having her sister with her at the Abby. She being your real foster sister I have desired Ally to give her a situation in the house.[19]

I hear from Maurice to day. He was prevented coming home for the last week by an alarm from the Abby that some suspicious looking men were seen about the place. On Sunday last he returned to the Abby, had an armed *force* on the watch for several Nights headed by himself but no attack was made. I suppose *Mick Kelly* formed one of the *defensive* body.

You will be glad to hear Phil Primrose's body was washed ashore on Wednesday Morning last close to where he sunk. Maurice says it was very little disfigured. It was brought to Killgrave in the coffin and on last

Thursday it was to have been interred. Though this circumstance renews the grief of his afflicted Parents yet it is a melancholy consolation to have the dear fellows remains laid in consecrated ground. There was to have been a high Mass celebrated on the day of interment at Carhen. Recollect my child to offer up the next Mass you repent at for the repose of the poor felows soul and ask Gregory to join you in that work of mercy.

Now to turn to a more pleasing subject. Poor Julia O Brien gave birth to a little *bit* of a son yesterday morning. She was but a short time ill. I saw her late yesterday as well as possible and so happy. I had her Son in my arms and I assure it was as Light as a baby. It is a nice looking Infant and I think like its Father. We may now call them the 'wee wee man, the wee wee Wife, the wee wee child with the wee wee house'. I cant say when he is to be christened or what his name is to be.

I suppose you read the advertisement from your brewery in the Pilot. The Sweatmans are greatly cried down for the meeting they had to try to put down the real Dan by underselling your establishment. It will eventualy destroy themselves.[20]

The Pilot also told you that your Father patronized a play on last Thursday Night and such a house I never saw. It was so crowded and of course so noisy we did not hear a word of the tragedy except part of each of the two last acts. Your Father was received at the doors with cheers all the way to the box and when he made his appearance there the cheering and waving of handkerchefs from the boxes and from every part of the house was beyond any thing you can form an idea. I often wished you were with us. I suppose you recollect the story on which the tragedy is founded.

The Costigans were prevented going to the Theatre by the illness and expected death of poor Mr Locby. He is now however better but cant live very long. John Costigan is gone to London. Sylvester is not yet come home.

I hope soon to hear from you at lenght that you are quite well and as happy as I could wish you to be at school and in favour with your Masters. Your Father will I am sure go see you at Christmas. This ought to induce you to be very studious and to distinguish yourself at the

Christmas Vacation. You know how much it delights your Father to have his sons exert the talents they were blessed with. Indeed they should leave nothing undone to prove themselves worthy of their Father. He is greatly pleased with John. He now works in the Study and gives his Father much satisfaction by the manner and rapidity with which he writes from his dictation opinions and also notes his briefs. Ffrench and Morgan quiz him very much on the opinions he writes. The other day Stranger was assaulted by one of Mrs Sprads [?] dogs. A case is to be laid before John for his opinion and he is to be counsel for the Plaintiff *Strangy*.

I got your round of Beef yesterday prepared for spicing. How did you like the Turkey and ham. Did the bottle of Rasberry Vinegar go safe. How are your bowels.

[remainder missing]

36. *Mary O'Connell to Daniel O'Connell Jr*

Wednesday [November 1831]

My dear Danny

I got your letter on Monday and waited answering it with the hope I should be able to tell you dear Maurice was come home. I have not heard from him this week but am every moment expecting the happiness of seeing him. The inclosed from the Tralee paper will tell you poor Phils funeral has taken place. God comfort his poor family and have mercy on his soul. Pray for him my dearest child.

Why should you think it necessary to ask for permission to take tea at your breakfast. If not against rule take it also in the evening as well as in the morning if you wish for it.

Your Secretary Mr [P. V.] Fitzpatrick was here this morning. He gave a pleasing account of the result of the sale of your porter last Monday. The Drays and horses were the admiration of those who saw them and they were cheered through every street when they passed. The Men are most comfortably dressed and on the shafts of the Drays are a large brass plate with a shamrock on it and Daniel Ô Connell Junior and Co in large letters on it. I have ordered a hogshead of the porter to be sent here that the servants should drink your health in your own porter this Christmas. There is every prospect of the rapid success of this new establishment. You will please God by the time you come of age be a rich Man. Then I hope you will find it your interest to take an active part in the establishment without at all taking from your consequence as a Gentleman.

Your Father bids me tell you with his love you may depend upon his going to see you on a Saturday and stopping until the following Monday probably your elder brothers may accompany him. John does not like going to Clongows. He has not yet given his opinion on *Strangy's* Case.

We heard to day from Ellen. She and her babes are quite well so is FitzSimon. Julia and her boy are going on very well. I believe she means to Nurse him. He is to be called after you and you are to be named God-Father John standing for you with your Mod as GodMother. The christening will I believe take place next Sunday if Julia will be strong enough to bear the bustle. There are none to be present but this family. The little fellow will be the image of his Father who is quite proud of his *Son* and *heir*. Julia would prefer a daughter who would have been my namesake.

While I write Kate is talking trash to Stranger. James told me that a Woman who keeps a public house told him that if she had six hogsheads of the *real Dan* she would have sold them all yesterday.

Morgan Ô Connell did not tell me any thing about the message about the tea. He seems pleased with Clongows and I should not be surprised if his brother Maurice was to be sent *there*.

I have no news for you. Dublin is as stupid as it can possibly be. We *all* dine today at Mr Powers in Harcourt Street. It is to be a great time out.

Do you get the Pilot newspaper. I asked you this question before and you did not answer it. I ordered it to be sent to you regularly. Are your bowels quite well. We have no cholera here and there is very little of it in London. The Physicians here say it wont come to Dublin until next June. As you will see the account of poor Phils funeral apeared into the Pilot. I shant send the extract from the Kerry.

All our friends in Kerry are quite well. Your Cousin Dan Ô Connell has joined his Regiment at Chatham. I hope soon to get your cousin little Jimmy Ô Connell on the bars [?] of the Irish College in Paris. He is a clever boy. His sister Betsy is at school at Miss Arrtaynes [?] in Killarney and your aunt her Mother is now living near Killorglin with her cousin Lady Blennerhassett who is a Catholic and her husband a convert to the Catholic faith. Unfortunately they have no children.

[*remainder missing*]

37. *Mary O'Connell to Daniel O'Connell Jr*

Saturday the 25th [November 1831][21]

My dearest Danny

Maurice has not arrived and until I shall actually see him in the house I will not believe he is thinking of coming home. He got to Tralee on Wednesday last being obliged to sleep at Miltown the Night before as the horses that came to the carriage that brought him and Ellen Connor tired and could not be got to go to Tralee that night. Maurice O Connor they left in attendance upon old Mrs Muhoney of Arghada [?] who was dying. She came to see the poor family at Killgrave and was taken so suddenly ill at Mrs Creeghs when she stopped they could not remove her to lodgings.

Poor Phils remains were interred on Thursday week. Nothing could have been more melancholy than the funeral procession. Maurice walked arm in arm with the Knight of Kerry and during the procession to the Church of Cahirsivine and the interment of the poor fellows remains minute Guns were fired from the Yacht. Ricarda Primrose says she fears old Mrs Primrose will never recover from Phils untimely fate. She has not left her room since the day the fatal event took place — the Girls and their poor Father and brother are in the greatest affliction. Ricardas sweet Baby is the only consolation they have. Her attempts to talk and her little tricks amuse them when they can be brought to think of any thing besides their misfortune.

I saw Julia today. I took her a present of a christening cup for young Master. He has become very stout and she is suckling him herself of which she is very proud. He is to be made a christian of tomorrow at two o clock by Mr Whelan of Townsend Street. Mr Whelan your friend and Mr L'Estrange are to be present. John is to stand for you. Mr Simpson is to be the other Godfather and the Lady who lodges in the house the other GodMother. She is a protestant but that is of no matter when there is to be a Catholic Lady to hold and answer for the child. I shant close this letter until Monday when I shall give you an account of the Christening.

Monday. My dear Danny I have just got your letter and hope ere this reaches you will have quite got rid of the mumps. They are a painful but not a dangerous complaint. I once had them so bad that it was only by opening my mouth with a spoon I could take any food for an entire day and that food very soft.

Your Father returned this morning from Drogheda where he yesterday attended a charity sermon. He is quite well but as yet cant fix on the *precise* Saturday he will go see you. You shall have a *weeks notice* of the visit.

How did you get off this examination. I am told Mr Duncan says to every person that you are a spoiled child by *me*. I dont realy think I deserve he should speak of me in those terms and I should much regret you giving him cause to make this ill notioned remark upon your Mother. He should learn a *little discretion*. Tell him I spoke to you on this one disagreeable subject. I should wish him to know I have heard of his *kindnes*.

We had a great Christening yesterday. Your humble servant and you represented by John, Mr Simpson and a Mrs Williams who live at Julia's the Sponsors. The Company besides were Kate Betsy Bessy Edward Tuohy Mr L'Estrange and Mr Whelan of Townsend street who performed the ceremony. The little fellow was in grand costume. He cried a little but not when the water was thrown on his head. I would not tell Julia this for though a superstitious remark it would lead to make her unhappy. She only sat up yesterday for the first time in her room and got some chicken to eat. She is looking very well. The christening took place in the drawing room. He was called 'Daniel Joseph'. He is realy a pretty child. Not quite as big or as heavy as a large wax Doll. Julia is nursing him and she says she would not give her son for the Kings dominions. She hopes he will have a situation in your brewery one of these days.

The brewery is going on very well. We had some of your porter yesterday at dinner. They all said it was very good. In honour of you I took a drink of it to your health and the servants say it is the best porter they every drank. With your next prog I shall send you a few bottles of the porter. I shall also send you wax Candles. How am I to send you the papers and some Christening cake Julia gave me for you.

Maurice is not yet come back. I suppose he will be here this evening. Some letters came directed to him to day from Tralee. I suppose the Dewitts stopped him in Limerick yesterday.

Alicia is happy as her heart can wish her. She is living at their country place. They are to be in Dublin for the next term. You will be glad to hear Ian O Connells wife is becoming a Catholic. She is under the care and religious instructions of the Nuns.

[*remainder missing*]

38. *Mary O'Connell to Daniel O'Connell Jr*

Tuesday the 29th [November] 1831

My dearest Danny

I was out yesterday when Morgan John called which I regret as I had many questions to ask him. One amongst the many if it was possible that the boys were stript to be flogged. This practice has been long given up in every publick school and I can hardly think the Jesuits would be behind in the work of civilization. Even from the army flogging is now quite abolished. I wish to have it in my power to contradict this report as I should regret any circumstance that would injure the establishment at Clongows. My feeling is that if a boy is base enough to deserve a flogging he should be expelled [from] the college. To you I trust there is no

fear such a disgraceful punishment should be ever resorted to. Your dis-
position is naturally good and affectionate. You are also religious and you
have talents that ought if properly applied render you incapable of
deserving any punishment. I trust my dear Danny you are making up for
the long and pleasant vacation you have had by applying yourself with
diligence to your studys and doing every thing in your power to gratify
your indulgent Father and merit the esteem of your Masters and those
in authority over you. How it would grieve your Father were he to hear
that you were idle at school and deserved punishment of any kind. Flogging of course is out of the question. I should hardly think that even Mr.
O'B who was by what every boy says who ever was at Clongows very
fond of administering the Cat of Nine tails would be now allowed to per-
severe in that base and cruel kind of punishment.

Who is your present Master and what are you learning. At your age
my dear Danny you should be very dilligent and conscious to improve
yourself. You are no longer a child and you should take every advantage
to profit by the time [?] you may have [?] to stop at school. I know you
are sometimes inclined to idle and to be too fond of your own care and
comfort and you have also my dear child a fault which you should correct. It is an irritability in your temper that sometimes induces you to
give rude answers which in cool reflection you afterward are so sorry
for. More than once while in London you answered me pertly and I
assure you I felt it very much particularly coming from you. To your
brothers and sisters you likewise spoke rudly. This manner my dear
child will steal upon you and make you disagreeable to your friends and
make yourself eventualy unhappy. I got your *last* letter and cannot take
notice of the subject of it without incurring for you much of your
Fathers displeasure.

We are all quite well. The Fitzsimons left us on Sunday. Maurice is
not yet come home. I heard from him yesterday. He desired me tell you
with his love that Mick Kelly has paid his May rent and half of this
November rent. He has a *Son* of Jack Darlings rearing for you. I dont
know *the Mother*.

James Connor was not able to go see you. He was very ill last week and left Dublin last Night in the Mail for home. Poor fellow was very delicate.

Let me know if you get the basket safe. How are your bowels. If they still continue delicate you ought not to take any of the Rasberry Vinegar or any fruit or sweetmeats. Let me hear from you in reply to this.

I believe Ffrench will go down to see you before he leaves this. Your Father will probably go down about Christmas as he will not go to London this session. With love from your Father sisters and Brothers. Ever believe me your fond Mother. Take care of yourself.

Mary Ô Connell

39. *Mary O'Connell to Daniel O'Connell Jr*

[15 December 1831]

My dearest Danny

I have been anxious expecting to hear from you for though you said the Mumps were not painful I wish to know if you are quite well. Gregory does not say any thing on the subject in his letters to his Mother. This week he says he got very well over the examination. Better than he expected. How did you get through your examination.

Maurice returned this morning. He is quite well and healthy looking much fater than when I saw him this day eight weeks. He gives me a great account of Jack who he says is become very fat. His Son is a very nice animal. His Mother is a Mare of Mick Kelly's. Your boat is in great order and laid up in Maurices boat house. Your Seaman is a right good one. He is Jack Connells third Son. Ally is a great housekeeper and your foster sister is living also at the Abbey. Maurice says the trees are growing fast and the place looking very handsome. I hope we shall all be able to judge of the beauty of the Abbey.

The Session next Spring will be over early in July — please God. It is thought the reform bill will pass the next Session. For England the Scotch reform bill takes precedence of the Irish. The latter will give the Government and Ministers more trouble than they expect. Your Fathers speech at the political meeting will give them reason to suppose they must give up their idea of humbugging the Irish people much longer.[22] I wish we had our Irish parliament here before two years come about.

Your Father is if possible more popular than ever he was and as to your brewery nothing can equal the sale they can have for the porter. The people will not drink any but the real Dan every one says. The future success of the Brewery is certain. By the time please God you are of age you will have a very fine independence and I trust you will meet your Father's wishes of attending to the establishment yourself. The inclosed ballads will amuse you. They are continually sung through all the streets and *your* Drays continue to be cheered as they pass along with the porter.

FitzSimon came to Town yesterday to take proceedings against James Mahon for a libel. You must have read his attack upon FitzSimon at the county meeting and Fitz reply to him. Mahon afterwards put an article in one of the papers saying Mrs Christopher FitzSimon had the audacity to come to the county meeting and to contradict the charges made by him of FitzSimons having forged the *Irish* resolutions which he again asserted were forged by him.

The babes have I fear got the Measles. They were ill when their Father left yesterday Morning particularly O Connell who is generally more heavily attacked by any illness than any of the other children. Something like your brother John when a child.

Maurice spent four days at his Cousins Alicia Dewitts near Castle Connell. He says she is as happy as possible and a great favourite to her papa and Mama in law. She is to come to Dublin with her husband next term. I believe her sister Mary is to come with her.

I have no news for you indeed Dublin affords no subject. Nor is it likely to do so. How are you getting on at *school*. I hope my child you are conscientiously attentive to your studys. At your age it is necessary not to lose a moment while at your studies to improve your self in every point of education. Who is your Latin Master. Do you like him as well as you did Mr O Farrell.

Mr. Nicholson is always asking for you. He talks of going down to see you. I am sorry to say he is again very delicate. Your little bird is quite well. The other birds are quite well in comparison to him. He is

a great pet to all of us. He knows your Father quite well — with love
from all your friends here believe me my dear child your fond Mother

Mary Ô Connell

40. *Mary O'Connell to Daniel O'Connell Jr*

[December 1831]

My dearest Danny

I had the pleasure of hearing of you yesterday from Mr Esmond who
was kind enough to call upon me. I was afraid to ask him many questions about you lest he may upbraid me for giving you so long a Vacation. How did you get off this examination. You will know this evening.

Your Father has settled to go down to see you on this day fortnight
and to stop until the following Monday. Maurice will certainly accompany him and I believe Morgan the day which he goes down to see the
FitzSimons. I fear to go lest I might suffer by going to the country this
time of the year.

The little children are now quite well. I have not a word of news to
tell you. Did you hear lately from Ally. I sent on your last letter to her.

You will be sorry to hear Kate will not be able to ride her Mare any
more. She is unsafe for her. Morgan now rides her. Kate and Morgan
accompany Betsy to Fort William early in the next Month and I fear
your Father Maurice and myself will be delayed to go to London. We
shall please God be back before Easter and have the pleasure of seeing
you *somewhere*. Hanna and James stop here with your brother John. I
believe I shall take Bessy O'Connell as a companion with me and Eliza
as a Maid. Old Richard I shall send to the Abby with the horses and take
only John with me.

We had a dinner party the other day. The Powers of Harcourt Street
and the Balfs with some people in the evening. I was dead tired the next
day it was so long a time since I entertained a large party before. Thank
God I am quite well so is your dear Father. You may depend upon getting the prog by him.

[*remainder missing*]

41. *Mary O'Connell to Daniel O'Connell Jr*

[17 December 1831]

My dear Danny

I write to you to day for the purpose of sending you the inclosed letter from I believe James Connor. The invitation to Ffrench from *you* and the firm your Father and your brothers also got. They will all go and drink your health. The envious people gave out that your Father had no connection at all with the establishment and to refute this Calumny he has accepted their and your invitation to a dinner to celebrate the opening of the brewery which is succeeding beyond the expectations of your friends.

You will hear from Gregory of poor Mr. Locbys death. He is to be interred on Monday. Maurice will go to the funeral in my carriage as we wish to pay every respect to the memory of our Learned friend.

Fitzsimon left yesterday for home. He regretted he could not dine with you and your firm. The little ones are a good deal [better?]. I hope they will escape the measles until a more mild season.

I am glad to find you are quite well. You need not say any thing either to Mr Duncan or to any other person on the subject of my last letter but one.

Nothing new here. I heard from Mama B yesterday. She is quite well and desires her fond love to you. She loves you very very much. What became of the knife I gave you. I shall attend to what you wish respecting the prog.

Why did you not tell me Mrs Kelly of Aeten had the kindness to ask for you the day she visited Clongows. Were you allowed to stay with her for any time. Her daughters governess told me she saw you.

I suppose you will be soon going to your Xmas duty. I hope my child you dont forget to pray for your brother Maurice who I am happy to tell you is stedfast in his intention of going to Communion as soon as his Director allows him. With fond love from your Father your Sisters, Bessy and Ffrench. Believe me your fond Mother.

                                        Mary Ô Connell

42. *Mary O'Connell to Daniel O'Connell Jr*

Saturday Night [January 1832]

My darling Danny —

I cant tell you how much annoyed I was that your Father was not able to go to Clongows to day as he first intended. You will however be glad to see him and dear Maurice. You may depend upon being brought up at Easter.

I got your message from Mr Whelan and shall attend to it. In the mean time do you be very dilligent and well prepared for the examinations before Easter.

In the basket I believe you will find every thing you asked for. The Beef is better than a round and more fit for keeping. In the Jar is port Wine Vinegar. You have Sugar, Sugar Candy, Liquerice ball all kinds of Comfits, Christening Cake and twelfth Night Cake Oranges Apples Nuts and Figgs and six Spirmiatta [?] candles, paper, blotting paper and sealing Wax.

You did not tell me if you liked your Knife. I hope you will take every care of it and not either sell it or give it away. Should you want any thing more let me know but I do not think you do. Good Night my dear Child. Your Father will give you a great many kisses for your Mod

Mary Ô Connell

43. *Mary O'Connell to Daniel O'Connell Jr*

Merrion Square
January the 12th [1832]

My dearest Danny

In the full expectation of hearing from you according to your message I waited to write in reply to your favour which as yet I have not received. I hope you are not prevented by illness from writing to some one of your correspondents here.

Your Father and Maurice arrived on Monday before Eleven o clock. Need I say my child how pleased I was with the good account they each gave me of you. Your dear Father seems greatly pleased with you but hopes you will every day become more sensible and steady and more attentive to your studys. Your Masters are pleased with you in fact you appear to be a general favourite to all the Gentlemen and believe me my dear Danny this information is a great source of comfort to your Mod. I hope my dear Danny you will checque the little faults of temper which you have and also that indolence and laziness which you too often give way to. I trust most sincerely that you will verify your Father's prophecy of you which is as follows. 'My sweet Danny will be a great comfort to us when he returns from school. He has good sense great energy good abilitys and a wish to make his Father and Mother happy.' May the great God bless you my darling boy and give you the grace to fulfil your fond Father's expectations.

I believe we shall be leaving this on Sunday next. It is thought there will be a long winter Recess and at all events the entire two Sessions will be over before the first of July.

Your request to Mr Whelan shall be granted in the way you wish but keep your mind to yourself. I dare say Mrs Costigan will also grant Gregorys request on the same subject. There was a large ball at *his* house last Monday. I did not go. Betsy Kate and Morgan leave on Sunday for Fort William. Ffrench is now there preparing the house for their reception. John stays here and I hope will go to see you. Hanna and James also stay here so that if you want any thing you have only to write for it. How did you like your prog.

FitzSimon is in Town. He left them all well. Mary is become a Barker. She barked two dolls I sent her by Kate. Julia is quite well and her little boy thriving.

We heard to day from Tralee. All well there. Your brewery is getting on famously. Nothing drank but the real Dan. You will make a fortune every person says. Old Richard is going to the Abby. He has got a new name. The (Exile of S[*illegible*]) from having remarked that we were sending him to S[*illegible*] when we fixed on sending him to the Abbey. I shall write to you again on Saturday. We have very bad weather here. Constant rain.

You will read in the Pilot a great attack on your Father from Lord Cloncurry and another from Doctor Doyle. Your Father means this day to answer (in his speech at the political meeting) Doctor Doyle and he is writing an answer to Lord Cloncurry. What a shame for a Dignitary of the Church of Christ to attack with such virulence one of the props [?] of the Church by his example and his piety and charity.[23] I dare say Mr Esmond will be quite amazed at it and Mr O Connor. Good by my dearest Danny. Believe me always your fond Mother

Mary Ô Connell

44. *Mary O'Connell to Daniel O'Connell Jr*

[16 January 1832]

My darling Danny

I got your letter this morning and for this time forgive you. Do my child in future write to me every week direct your letters 4 Parliament Street. We start tomorrow as my cold is quite gone and I am myself again. I hope to hear from you the day of my arrival Saturday next under care to Maurice that you are quite rid of your cold.

Betsy Kate Morgan and *Stranger* left to day for Fort William. We miss Kate very much but it was right she should go with Betsy for some time. She stays until before Easter when please God *we* shall *all* meet here. I trust in health and happiness in the mean time.

I beg of you my dear child to be very attentive to your studies and make up for last time. Do my dear Child be sensible. You are now approaching Manhood and get over all your little failings and you will be all your fond Parents can wish.

I heard this day from Ally. She got your last letter and will soon write to you. All the news she mentions is the sad news of poor Peg the Washerwomans death who lived at the gate Lodge. She died in child birth may God have mercy upon her.

I must now my Child conclude. I have so much to do. Pray for us in particular for Maurice who is to go tomorrow to Communion. With

love from your Father Bessy and her brothers. Believe me always your
fond Mother

Mary Ô Connell

Monday Night

45. *Mary O'Connell to Daniel O'Connell Jr*

Llangathen Wednesday
Evening 7 oclock [18 January 1832]

My darling Danny

    We got from the head last Night about half past Eleven after a very
excellent passage. None of our party sick but Bessy and she very little
so. Thank God I am quite stout much better than when I left home yesterday. It was too late for me to write to you last Night. You shall hear
again from London as soon as I get there which wont be until late on
Friday. I often thought of you these two days so did your Father. I miss
Kate very much but she is better off where she is than at Number 4 Parliament Street London. Stranger is gone also on a visit to Fort William.
Your Uncle Finn promised me to go see you so did Mr. L'Estrange but
not at the same time.

    I must now bid you good by. With love from your Father Maurice
and Bessy. Believe me always my darling Danny your fond Mother

Mary O Connell

46. *Mary O'Connell to Daniel O'Connell Jr*

Friday the 20th [January 1832]
Birmingham
One o clock afternoon

    My darling Danny has I hope got my letter from the head. We are
but just arrived here all quite well. We slept last Night at Wolverhampton. Three miles beyond that Town *we* were met by the Political
Union and the people with Music and banners and thus escorted to the
hotel where a deputation waited on your Father with an address which

he answered in his usual style. Afterwards went on the balcony and addressed the Multitude who received him with deafening applause. He is now gone with Maurice to attend and speak at the political Union meeting in this Town. Immediately after we start from here and go as far as we can this way escorted by the people from this place with music and banners. We shall arrive too late tomorrow to write by the post from London. Therefore these few lines will tell you all is right. You shall soon hear from me again.

I Inclose this to John. Recollect your promise of writing once every week. With love from your Father from Maurice and Bessy believe me darling Danny your fond Mother

Mary Ô Connell

I write in great haste for the post

47. *John O'Connell to Daniel O'Connell Jr*

Saturday 28th Jany 1832

My dear Danny

I hope you received two letters from *Mod* which she enclosed to me. I had them sent without delay to the office. I need not tell you anything about her as you have I dare say heard from her since the date of my last which was the 19th instant.

I have heard from Roscommon twice. All friends there are very well. Kate likes the country very much and admires Betsy's place extremely. Betsy is quite a *woman of business* now, going about with her *own* keys, ordering dinner and taking care of her *own* house. Morgan has had some very good hunting and expects a good deal more as soon as I can get his top boots out of Tobin's hands and send them down to him.

I frequently see your friends Coffey & Hearne who both seem quite well. The latter was one of the company that received us at your brewery, the day my father, Maurice, Morgan, Ffrench & I dined there. Your porter is certainly very good and is, I hear on all hands, everywhere sought for. By the bye as we *promised* to *dine* with you often when you take up the management yourself, you must give us better wine than your partners did. We wont patronize you if you give us Cape Madeira and execrable Sauterne.

Remember me to Greg and tell him all his people are quite well. I saw them yesterday. I am sorry you & he did not see the lions, boa constrictors, pelican &c &c that have been on the stage here. There was less of humbug in the thing than is usual in such exhibitions, for there was a good deal of real danger to the owner of the animals who pulled the lions about & played with them as if they were dogs. They certainly *acted their parts* in the sort of play in which they were introduced, exceedingly well & showed wonderful docility. The baboon rather over-acted his part for he seized on a standard that a man carried in one of the processions and they had to beat the unfortunate creature before he would let go his hold.

I have just had a note from Ellen. She and the children are quite well. FitzSimon is in town, brought up I believe by the necessity of attending Court to watch the progress of his suit against Mahon.

Goodbye my dear Danny. I have nothing more to say but that I am your truly loving brother

John Ô Connell

48. *Mary O'Connell to Daniel O'Connell Jr*

[London]
Monday Morning [30 January 1832]

My dearest Dannys letter of the last Friday week or Monday last I got this morning. You dated Friday the 23^d. Monday was the 23^d. I assure you I was delighted when I saw a prospect of frost but I fear it is now all over and that I shant have the comfort of knowing you have been able to skaite but my child you must be very careful and cautious of not going too far and of not getting cold. I have got Maurice to write to Mr Connor to beg he will have your cough attended to and to gratify me my dear Child I am sure you will not refuse to wear

Worsted Stockings until the beginning of April and a piece of flannel to your chest.

Have you had any return of the pain you complained of last Spring when you had a cough. Have you got the blankets on your bed that I sent with you when last going to school. You must take every precaution against cold and damp in the feet. Wear very thick shoes.

I heard to day from Ellen Kate and John. The latter said he would write to you that post. FitzSimon is now in Dublin settling with O Mara about Glencullen. Ellen hopes they will be settled there before Easter. They intend letting Ballinamena. They have had many applications for it. The children are all well very much grown and Christy very fond of the *tea pop* as he calls tea pot. Mary has got long *treses* of which she is very proud. O Connell is a sweet child very gentle and very handsome.

Kate is quite delighted with Fort William. It is she says a most pretty place and they are as pleasant as possible to be. She rides a very nice Mare belonging to Ffrench and Morgan hunts twice a week on a hunter of Ffrenchs. They have gone about very much and Betsy is quite a nice little Lady of a house. Instead of punning Morgan and Ffrench have taken up making rhymes for every word that is said. *They* are a merry pair. Stranger is very well and enjoys the country greatly.

All your friends have enquired very kindly for you. Poor Baldwin is confined since we came here by some painful illness. He is now better. Doctor Jarsy [?] is getting into business. He is in attendance on Colonel D'Exter the Duke of Sussexs Son. This will be of use to him. Lord Kilmallock is about being married to a young Lady who has taken a fancy to him. She has four hundred a year and two thousand pounds and great expectations from an old rich Uncle. If Kilmallock is married he will not go to Belany bay as long as he can keep away from it. I have seen him but twice since we came. He is taken up with his Lady love.

We have got a very comfortable house here and so welcome. We are next door to Madam *Millet*. The O Connor Dons lodge there. Mrs Hughs and Emma enquired particularly for you. Emma has mentioned a [*two illegible words*]. Dan O Connell dined here yesterday. He is much improved and likes his new situation very well. He told me yesterday he heard from a brother officer of Maurice O Connell (the Generals son) that he was in a conscription. He is with his Regiment at Germany. Your Grandmama is very well but poor Aunt Chute is very bad. All our other friends in Tralee and *Kerry* are all well.

I hope you got the Pilot paper regularly. It is this day announced that the Queen is in a fine way to give an heir to the crown. I hope so to keep out the Duke of Cumberland.[24]

It is thought the reform bill will pass. They will have a great battle about the Irish bill. Your Father will fight it out with them.

Bessy bids me tell you with her love she will soon write to you again. She likes London very much. She is great company to me. Betsy Mahony is here and desires love to you.

It was not at Llangathen we slept going back to Dublin it was *Cornil Ogee* [?]. Llangathen is the smaller Town near the beautiful Vale you admired so much. Do your recollect how you pounded poor Bligh in that journey.

I have given you all the news here. You will be glad to hear poor Shiel is able to come out every day. He will soon be quite at liberty. He is looking very well. Your Father and Maurice unite in love to you my dear child with your ever fond and attached Mother

Mary O Connell

49. *Mary O'Connell to Daniel O'Connell Jr*

[London]
[1 March 1832]

My dearest Danny

Bessee is about writing so long a letter to you I shall only tell you your dear Father left this yesterday for Ireland where he hopes he will be early on Saturday next. He proposes God willing to *breakfast* with you on Tuesday Morning next the 6th of March on his way to Kilkenny. Tell him I beg of you the real state of your health if the pain in your side is quite gone which side is afflicted and how the cough is and how long you have had it. You say [to?] Betsy the pain is surely gone. I hope you will take the pills ordered by Jarsey [?] for you and that you will write to him under cover to me exactly what he wishes you to write and dont exercise too much or expose yourself to cold.

Have you and Gregory as yet made up your minds as to the plan I recommend to you of stopping at school until the long vacation. If you do so I have not a doubt Mrs Costigin will allow Gregory to come with you to the Abby. We hope to be there early in July and I would recommend to you and to Gregory to start at once for the Abby when your vacation commences. That is to say going first to Dublin to see Mrs Costigan and then coming to Cork in the Steam packet. As soon as you make up your mind about stopping at school until August I shall write to Mrs Costigan and make your Father apply to [her?] for leave for Greg to go with you to the Abby before he leaves Dublin the end of this Month.

I often see your friend Hurt [Hunt?]. He is very well. John does not like London or any thing in it not even the Theatres. He is '*the pleasantest fellow in the world*'. Ever your fond Mother

Mary O'Connell

You may *surely* reckon on seeing your Father on Tuesday next the 6th of March. He promised me to go on *that* day please God.

50. *Mary O'Connell to Daniel O'Connell Jr*

Thursday [9 March 1832]

My dearest Danny

I got your letter yesterday certainly not calculated to calm my mind as with the continued pain in your side. You complain of pain in the back and shortness of breathing also of your bowels. Was it for the latter you took medicine and were confined to the Infirmary and what kind of medicine. You took I hope not salts as they are considered extremely injurous to the bowels and stomach. You should be cautious about what you eat such as oranges apples sweet things of all discription and salt Fish. I hope you have leave for meat this lent. I have not seen Jarsy [?] since I got your last but I beg of you to attend to his advice and take the pills regularly and let him know through me the effects of them as to the removal or amoleration of the cough and pain of the side and back.

How I do long to hear from your Father. He promised to write to me from Kilkenny on his arrival there from Clongows last Tuesday and to give me a full and true account of you. I cannot however expect his letter before tomorrow if indeed I get it then. However I shall delay this letter with the hope of being able to tell you tomorrow I have heard of you through your Father.

Saturday. My darling Danny. It was only this morning I had the happiness to get your Father's first letter from Kilkenny, he having arrived there from Clongows after the post had left for Dublin. Your dear Father is quite well. He writes in great spirits about you. Tells me you are grown tall and thin that your cough is nothing and the pain you complained of was under your ribs and not in the side. That you made a ravenous breakfast on roast Turkey the morning he got to Clongows. Notwithstanding all this my dear Child I beg of you to take the pills by Jarsys [?] *recipe* and to attend to his instructions if you wish to make my mind easy about your health and write to me every week without fail.

Your Father speaks of visiting you on his return to Dublin. Have you and Greg as yet determined what you would do about going *home* at Easter. I think you would be wise to be advised by me and adopt the plan I mentioned to you some time back.

I heard to day from Kate. They are all quite well. Morgan has taken of[f] his *Mus*taches. I also heard from dear Ellen. She and her babes are quite well. Mary must have a story told her every day by her Mama of what you did and said when you were a little *Baby*. Ô Connell is continualy speaking of you. He is becoming very stout. The other day his Mama called him a *Baby* and he looked quite indignant and at the housemaid coming into the room he desired her give his Mama a good beating in her *lap* with the *brush*. Christy is a great darling. Mary is become very tall most anxious to read. She makes great attempts to spell. I fear they will not get Glencullen after all from O Mara at least not time enough to move there before Ellens confinement next May. They could let Ballinamena at once if they wished.

John dislikes London very much and does not think it a handsome city. He is attending Mr Lynchs Chambers with Dewitt and learning the law. Alicia lodges in this street. She is very happy for Sister Mary is now with her Aunt Finn. They say Phrey is to [be] married to Miss Galway. I wish he was as she is a very nice Girl.

Old Primrose his Wife and daughters are going to live in Cork. Killgrave is to be John Primroses. I think we will be all welcome to Ricarda. Ally is now in full command at the Abby. She has got rid of her plague Moore but I am very sorry she *struck* him. Julias child your Father tells me has not got bigger since I saw him but he is pretty and thriving. I have not seen Jarsy [?] since I got your letter. Poor Baldwin has got a slow fever and ague.

We are all quite well but very lonely. Maurice made a great speech in reply to Lord Melter on the tithe question last Thursday Night. John was in the house and was delighted with Maurice as well as with the manner he was received and attended to. He was also very much cheered. I wish I had been listening to him. He is continualy in the house since his Father left Town.

John and Sylvester Castigan are here still. Hurt [Hunt?] is gone to Winchester. I believe Letitia Costigan is to go to Betsy very shortly.

I must now my dear Danny conclude this letter with love from your brothers Bessy and Betsy Mahoney. Christy O Connell has left London. He has I believe got his commission for his brother Dan. I have no London news for you only we are not at all afraid of the Cholera. Believe me with love to Greg My dear child your fond Mother

Mary Ô Connell

Aunt Chute is still very ill. Mama B quite well but unhappy about Aunt Chute.

51. *Mary O'Connell to Daniel O'Connell Jr*

[London]
[20 March 1832]

My dearest Danny

Since your Father left this we have got but one letter from you. You should my child be careful not to let a week pass without writing once either to me or to Bessey. Consider the distance between us and what a pleasure it is to me to hear often from you. Besides I am anxious to hear the result if Jarsys [?] prescription of the pain in your side is relieved by the Pills as well as the Cough and if you find the Jersy Frock of service. By the by I hope you have the blankets I sent with you on your bed.

We are all well here but dont know when your Father Kate and Morgan will be with us. Your Father had a great entry into Clonmel last Thursday and had a splendid one last Sunday to Cork. He is in the best health and spirits and proposes paying you a visit on his return from Cork and if possible of sleeping at Clongows the Night of his visit to you.

I had a letter to day from Kate. They are all well except Betsy who is delicate but there is a *reason* for it. I heard yesterday from Ellen. Poor little Christy has had another attack of convulsions but was quite well. The other darlings are in the best health.

I suppose you heard of the death of poor Maurice Primrose in America. He died the same week poor Phil was drowned and his Wife died in three days after him both of consumption. Dan Primrose was only recovered from a fever when he wrote home where he is expected.

How do you get on this lent. I hope you are allowed to eat Meat every day but the three prohibited in the diocese of Dublin. Are you glad there will be leave given in Dublin after Lent to eat meat on *all* Saturdays. Please God we shall enjoy that privilege at the Abby.

I cant say when we shall set off from this. The Reform bill is to go to the Lords on Monday and in another week we shall know its fate there. If it is thrown out they say we shall have had [*illegible*] England.

The moment there is the least likelihood of a Run [?] we shall be off for poor Ireland. Lord Grey has no energy neither has Lord Althorpe. How soon the bill would be answered if your Father was in either of their place.

Does Gregory often hear from home. Ellen complains that Catherine never writes to her. What a shame. Give my love to Gregory and tell him I hope to see him at the Abby this Summer. John is quite sick of London though he is the *pleasantest fellow* in it. Poor Watt Baldwin is only just recovered from a fever. I have not yet seen him. Kilmallock is not yet recovered. The old Uncle wont give the money. My dear child believe me your fond Mother

M Ô Connell

Fitzpatrick mentioned to Maurice last week that *your* Brewery is going on as well as it is possible. So is your Fathers tribute everywhere.

52. *Mary O'Connell to Daniel O'Connell Jr*

[London]
[29 March 1832]

[*attached to a letter from Bessy O'Connell to her cousin Danny*]

I would not let this Frank go without writing a few lines to my dearest Danny. I am not quite satisfied as you still complain though slightly of the pain in your side lower down than at first and of the continuance of the cough. I dont think much of *your* Apothecarys opinion as I dont know who he is. However your Father when he sees you will be a better judge how to act in having other advice for you. He is this day in Tipperary where he is to get a grand dinner.

I send you the last Tralee paper with a further account of the procession in Cork. Bessy has left nothing for me to say as to news. We are all quite well. I hope you dont fast much. Good by my dearest child. Betsy Mahony desires her love to you. You will probably see your Father in a day or two after this reaches you. You will I fear be not glad to see him in haste. Believe me your fond Mother

Mary Ô Connell

53. *Mary O'Connell to Daniel O'Connell Jr*

Dublin April the 28th 1832

My dearest Danny

You will be surprised to get a letter from me dated Dublin. I thought you were written to but find it was not the case. I came over by your Fathers desire as he thought we should be obliged to stop here three weeks longer but now find we cannot. John only came with me. Maurice is gone to Kerry and I left Bessy with Betsy Mahony in the house until my return.

I had a very bad passage of fifteen hours from the Head and the day before yesterday obliged to put back when seven hours at sea in consequence of the break of part of the Engine of the packet. Altogether we had a dreadful passage. I am quite well but dreadfully fatigued and to have the journey again to take in less than ten days is rather a horror to me.

I am all anxiety to see you. Say what day next week you would wish me to go see you. I will arrange it so as to be down at Clongows before twelve o clock and to stop until six in the Evening with you. Say if you wish for any thing that I can take to you. When we meet please God I shall talk to you on the subject of your last letter to me in London which I did not answer as Bessy talked of writing to you.

They are all here dreadfully alarmed about the cholera. Thank God there is none of it near Clongows. We will please God be able to go to the Abby this Summer as your Father says positively he will not stay beyond the end of June in London. I shall settle with Mrs Costigan to have Gregory accompany you and you may depend upon getting a good long vacation. Your Father is a little nervous about the cholera. He is however quite well. So is Kate Morgan and John who unite in fond love to you.

Write to me on receipt of this. I suppose you heard of poor Mr. Bernard<'s> death by < . . . > fall from his horse < . . . > this

morning. I have not yet [seen the?] Costigans. They are all well. Tel<l]
[Gre>gory with my love I saw his brother John <la>st Sunday in London. Sylvester was < . . . > little relapsed. I also saw your friend Mr
< . . . > in London very often. With love from your Father believe
me my dear child always your fond Mother

Mary Ô Connell

Notes to Introduction

1   Donal McCartney, 'The World of Daniel O'Connell' in Donal McCartney (ed.), *The World of Daniel O'Connell* (Dublin, 1980), p. 4.

2   Daniel O'Connell Jr was born in Dublin on 22 August 1816. He was the youngest child of Daniel and Mary O'Connell.

3   Clongowes Wood College, originally known as Castle Browne, was purchased by the Jesuits under the direction of Father Peter Kenney in 1814, in order to establish a college for the sons of Catholic gentry in Ireland. The castle was one of the border fortresses of the Pale during medieval times and dates back to the time of Henry VI. The college opened with 110 students amidst some criticism from Protestant journals as well as the Chief Secretary for Ireland, Robert Peel. However, within four years some 220 students were in attendance. See *The Irish Jesuit Directory* (Dublin, 1926), pp. 132–3.

4   The Costigans were family friends of the O'Connells. Gregory and Danny were the same age and attended Clongowes Wood College together. Mary O'Connell frequently consulted with Gregory's mother regarding the welfare of their young children. In addition, the families took turns visiting the boys or collecting them for vacations and holidays. On a few occasions Gregory spent his vacation with the O'Connells. Older Costigan children were also friends of Kate and John O'Connell and are often mentioned in the letters. It is unclear who exactly Gregory's parents were, but it can be assumed that his father was involved in politics, for the correspondence between Mary and Danny reveals that the family, like the O'Connells, travelled frequently between Ireland and England with the same regularity.

5   Bracketed numbers refer to the letters in this collection.

6   W. J. Battersby (ed.), *A Complete Catholic Directory, Almanack and Registry* (Dublin, 1836), p. 151.

7   Journal of Daniel O'Connell Jr: NLI, O'Connell Correspondence, MS 17882.

8   Ibid.

9   Ibid.

10 Nancy F. Cott, *The Bonds of Womanhood: 'Woman's Sphere' in New England, 1780–1835* (New Haven, 1977), p. 46; Judith Lewis, *In the Family Way: Childbearing in the British Aristocracy, 1750–1860* (New Brunswick, 1986), p. 62; Randolph Trumbach, *The Rise of the Egalitarian Family* (New York, 1978), p. 165.

11 Ellen O'Connell to Daniel O'Connell, 20 Mar. 1820: NLI, O'Connell Correspondence, MS 13645 (6).

12 Daniel O'Connell to Mary O'Connell, 12, 14 May 1825: NLI, O'Connell–FitzSimon Papers, microfilm P. 1621.

13 Trumbach, *Egalitarian Family*, pp. 238, 252–4; Lawrence Stone, *The Family, Sex and Marriage in England, 1500–1800* (London, 1977), p. 22.

14 Mary O'Connell to Daniel O'Connell, 1 Apr. 1820: NLI, O'Connell Correspondence, MS 13651 (21).

15 Cott, *Bonds of Womanhood*, p. 88.

16 Lenore Davidoff and Catherine Hall, *Family Fortunes: Men and Women of the English Middle Class, 1780–1850* (London, 1992), p. 398.

17 Ibid., p. 344.

18 Michael Durey, *The Return of the Plague: British Society and the Cholera, 1831–32* (Dublin, 1979), p. 2; S. J. Connolly, 'The "Blessed Turf": Cholera and Popular Panic in Ireland, June 1832', *Irish Historical Studies*, xxiii (1982–83), p. 215; see also R. J. Morris, *Cholera 1832: The Social Response to an Epidemic* (New York, 1976).

19 L. A. Clarkson, 'Love, Labour and Life: Women in Carrick-on-Suir in the Late Eighteenth Century', *Irish Economic and Social History*, xx (1993), p. 29. For a comparative study see Davidoff and Hall, *Family Fortunes*, p. 319. For a more extensive discussion of Mary O'Connell's domestic role and her use of correspondence in kin-keeping see Erin I. Bishop, 'The World of Mary O'Connell, 1778–1836' (Ph.D. thesis, University College, Dublin, 1996).

20 Donal McCartney, *The Dawning of Democracy: Ireland 1800–1870* (Dublin 1987), pp. 40–43.

21 For a more extensive discussion on the Act of Union and Emancipation see Thomas Bartlett, *The Fall and Rise of the Irish Nation: The Catholic Question, 1690–1830* (Dublin, 1992); D. George Boyce, *Nineteenth-Century Ireland: The Search for Stability* (Dublin, 1990); Fergus O'Ferrall, *Catholic Emancipation: Daniel O'Connell and the Birth of Irish Democracy, 1820–1830* (Dublin, 1985).

22 Boyce, *Nineteenth-Century Ireland*, p. 59; Oliver MacDonagh, 'O'Connell in the House of Commons' in McCartney (ed.), *World of Daniel O'Connell*, pp. 43–4. Quote from Daniel O'Connell, *Observations on Corn Laws, on Political Pravity and Ingratitude, and on Clerical and Personal Slander, in the Shape of a Meek and Modest Reply to the Second Letter of the Earl of Shrewsbury* (Dublin, 1842), p. 68, cited in Fergus O'Ferrall, *Daniel O'Connell* (Dublin, 1981), p. 68.

23 Oliver MacDonagh, *O'Connell: The Life of Daniel O'Connell, 1775–1847* (London, 1991), p. 315.

24 Boyce, *Nineteenth-Century Ireland*, p. 57; MacDonagh, *O'Connell*, p. 319.

25 *Freeman's Journal*, 13 Jan. 1831.

26 *The Pilot*, 19 Jan. 1831.

27 Ibid., 2 Feb. 1831.

28 *Hansard 3*, ii, 490–91, 609–13 (14–16 Feb. 1831); 1006–9 (28 Feb. 1831).

29 Boyce, *Nineteenth-Century Ireland*, p. 61; McCartney, *Dawning of Democracy*, pp. 120–21.

30 McCartney, *Dawning of Democracy*, p. 122; Daniel O'Connell to Mary O'Connell, 5 Mar. 1831: NLI, O'Connell–Fitz-Simon Papers, microfilm P. 1621.

31   *The Pilot*, 9, 11 May 1831; *Freeman's Journal*, 20 May 1831.

32   *The Pilot*, 23 May 1831.

33   MacDonagh, *O'Connell*, pp. 346–47; *Freeman's Journal*, 24 Jan. 1832.

34   McCartney, *Dawning of Democracy*, pp. 123–4; Gearóid Ó Tuathaigh, *Ireland before the Famine, 1798–1848* (Dublin, 1990), p. 169.

35   On 8 March 1832 Stanley moved the House of Commons to form a committee of the whole house on the tithe question. Charles Brownlow proposed an amendment, supported by Maurice O'Connell, that the debate over the issue be postponed until a full inquiry into the tithe question could be concluded by the select committee already appointed. The amendment was defeated by 313 to 31. See Letter 50; *Hansard 3*, x, 1331–42 (8 Mar. 1832).

36   Daniel O'Connell to P. V. Fitzpatrick, 21 Feb. 1833: *The Correspondence of Daniel O'Connell*, ed. M. R. O'Connell (8 vols, Shannon, 1972–80), v, 11.

37   McCartney, *Dawning of Democracy*, p. 124.

38   Patrick Lynch and John Vaizey, *Guinness's Brewery in the Irish Economy, 1759–1876* (Cambridge, 1960), pp. 90–91.

39   Ibid., pp. 91, 144.

40   Maurice R. O'Connell, 'O'Connell and his Family' in McCartney (ed.), *World of Daniel O'Connell*, p. 28.

41   Bishop, 'World of Mary O'Connell', pp. 39, 42–3.

42   Daniel O'Connell to Mary O'Connell, 28 Feb. 1831: NLI, O'Connell-Fitz-Simon Papers, microfilm P. 1621.

Notes to Narrative

1   Ellen O'Connell Fitz-Simon (12 Nov. 1805 – 27 Jan. 1883), first daughter of Daniel and Mary O'Connell and sister of Daniel O'Connell Jr. She married Christopher Fitz-Simon in 1825. Ellen resided with her husband and children at Ballinamena and later Glencullen in Co. Wicklow. Her children Mary, O'Connell and Christy appear frequently in the letters.

2   John O'Connell (20 Dec. 1810 – 24 May 1858), third son of Daniel and Mary O'Connell and brother of Daniel O'Connell Jr. John was the only O'Connell son who took a serious interest in politics. He too attended Clongowes, as well as Trinity College. In 1837 John was called to the bar. He first became an MP in 1832 and almost continually held a seat in parliament until 1857 (for Youghal 1832–37; Athlone 1837–41; Kilkenny City 1841–47; Limerick City 1847–51; Clonmel 1853–57). John married Elizabeth, daughter of Dr James Ryan, a medical practitioner of Bray, Co. Wicklow, in 1838. They had eight children.

3   Morgan O'Connell (31 Oct. 1804 – 20 Jan. 1885), second son of Daniel and Mary O'Connell and brother of Daniel O'Connell Jr. In June 1819 he purchased a commission in the Irish South American Legion. He also served in the Austrian army and returned to Ireland in 1830. In 1832 he was returned for Co. Meath and served as MP until 1840, at which time he became assistant registrar of deeds and, in 1846, registrar. In 1840 he married Kate Balfe. The couple had no children.

4   Born in Dublin but educated and ordained on the continent, Rev. William L'Estrange, O.D.C. (d. Dec. 1833) was provincial of the Irish Discalced Carmelites and prior of St Teresa's, Clarendon Street, Dublin. He served for many years as the O'Connell family's spiritual director.

5   Maurice O'Connell (27 June 1803 – 18 Oct. 1853), eldest child of Daniel and Mary O'Connell and brother of Daniel O'Connell Jr. Called to the bar in 1827, he had little time to build a legal career before his father had him elected as MP for Clare 1831–32 and for Tralee 1832–37, 1838–53. In 1832 he eloped with Frances Scott, with whom he had four children before their marriage became estranged.

6   Catherine (Kate) O'Connell (18 Mar. 1807 – 19 Apr. 1891), second daughter of Daniel and Mary O'Connell and sister of Daniel O'Connell Jr. She married her cousin Charles O'Connell of Kerry in 1832, with whom she had eight children.

7   Elizabeth (Betsey) O'Connell (21 Feb. 1810 – 3 Feb. 1893), third surviving daughter of Mary and Daniel O'Connell and sister of Daniel O'Connell Jr. In 1831 she married Nicholas Joseph Ffrench of Co. Roscommon and moved with him to his family home, Ffrench Lawn. In 1836 Ffrench was appointed stipendiary magistrate for Oughterard, Co. Galway. The couple had six children.

8   Edmund Kean (1787–1833), famous actor and tragedian. In June and July 1830 Kean appeared as Shylock in *The Merchant of Venice* at the Haymarket in London. See *DNB* entry; J. Fitzgerald Molloy, *The Life and Adventures of Edmund Kean, Tragedian, 1787–1833* (London, 1897), p. 393.

9   Slang term for food, similar to 'grub'; general provisions for a journey.

10 There are numerous references to 'franking' in the correspondence of the O'Connell family. It was a device by which mail could be transmitted free of charge if the envelope was endorsed, or 'franked', by the signature of a member of parliament. It is clear from the comments in Letters 21 and 22 that the family regarded it as a perquisite of social as well as economic value.

11 Henry Peter Brougham (1778–1868) was a barrister and an MP who served as Lord Chancellor from 1830 to 1834, during which time he carried out significant legal reform. His radical principles included parliamentary reform and the abolition of slavery.

12 Rev. Francis Joseph Nicholson (1803–55) joined the Discalced Carmelites in 1825. He served as a spiritual adviser to the O'Connell family. In 1852 he succeeded to the archbishopric of Corfu.

13 Newgate Prison, built in 1773 and located in Green Street, Dublin. Designed by
    Thomas Cooley (1740–84), it was neither well situated nor well built. Few ever
    escaped from it, and life inside was one of 'depravity and rot'. Described as 'a
    monument of inhumanity', it was demolished in the 1880s. See Maurice Craig,
    Dublin, 1660–1860 (Dublin, 1969), pp. 197–9.

14 Maurice O'Connell and the electors of Drogheda lodged two separate petitions
    against the return of John Henry North in the general election of August 1830 in
    which Maurice was defeated. On 3 March 1831 a committee decreed that
    North's election was valid. See *The Correspondence of Daniel O'Connell*, ed. M. R.
    O'Connell (8 vols, Shannon, 1972–80), iv, 284n.

15 These gifts of Orange regalia are curious. O'Connell's relationship with
    Orangeism began somewhat accidentally when, on 17 December 1796, a French
    invasion fleet sailed into Bantry Bay. Fearing attack, the city of Dublin reached a
    state of near panic. O'Connell, like many young professionals and law students,
    joined the Lawyers' Artillery Corps on 2 January 1797. Both professionally and
    personally speaking, it was an understandable move. Committed to the profes-
    sion, O'Connell felt he must adopt professional practices in order to gain accep-
    tance from his peers. In addition, the energy and activity of the yeomanry excited
    and attracted him. Yet politically his enlistment was perhaps strange. In combat-
    ing a possible French invasion, O'Connell was also aligning himself against the
    United Irish forces and the Catholic agrarian societies who were awaiting the
    arrival of these French reinforcements. He recorded in his journal his delight at
    participating in the corps drills and his fear of ending up on the wrong side of the
    revolution. He took a firm stance against revolution and radicalism, arguing that
    a revolution would not bring peace to Ireland and that moderation was the key to
    success. In the political turmoil of the day, however, the yeomanry moved further
    away from moderation, soon becoming a nest of radicals and Orangemen.
    O'Connell was caught in this period of uncertainty, turmoil and change and can
    in no way be accused of any type of duplicity in his support of and service to the
    Crown. Indeed, he feared and abhorred Orangeism, arguing against a political
    ascendancy based upon confessional allegiance. In later years O'Connell courted
    Protestant support for the Repeal movement. His stance on religious toleration
    and his alliance with the Whigs in promoting parliamentary reform perhaps
    explain these gifts. See Oliver MacDonagh, *O'Connell: The Life of Daniel O'Connell,
    1775–1847* (Dublin, 1991), pp. 52–6, 305; D. George Boyce, *Nineteenth-Century
    Ireland: The Search for Stability* (Dublin, 1990), pp. 58–64.

16 Barry Edward O'Meara (1786–1836) was born in Ireland and joined the British
    army in 1804 as an assistant surgeon. Dismissed from the army for assisting at a
    duel, he later joined the navy. While O'Meara was serving on HMS *Bellerphon*,
    Napoleon surrendered on board on 14 July 1815. On the invitation of the ex-

Emperor, O'Meara accompanied him to St Helena, where he acted as Napoleon's personal physician and surgeon. He was dismissed in 1818 for refusing to report on his private conversations with Bonaparte. In 1822 he published *Napoleon in Exile; or A Voice from St Helena*, which created a huge sensation and went into five editions. O'Meara died in 1836, purportedly after catching cold at one of O'Connell's meetings. See Henry Boylan, *A Dictionary of Irish Biography* (Dublin, 1978), pp. 275–6.

17 Patrick Vincent Fitzpatrick (1792–1865) was a personal friend and confidant of Daniel O'Connell. The son of the Catholic bookseller and publisher Hugh Fitzpatrick, he was educated at St Patrick's College, Maynooth, and became a member of the Irish bar. In the mid-1820s he joined the Catholic Association and was influential in persuading O'Connell to run for the 1828 by-election. In addition, Fitzpatrick took charge of raising funds for the campaign. Quickly becoming a favourite of O'Connell, he later served as O'Connell's political and financial adviser. Fitzpatrick's success in raising the national collections led him to oversee O'Connell's personal finances as well, which was no small matter, considering the extent of the Liberator's debt. Gradually he became a general adviser to the family, and, from the evidence of this collection of letters, it would appear that he acted as a secretary or assistant in charge of overseeing Danny's interest in the brewery. See MacDonagh, *O'Connell*, pp. 297–8.

18 John Primrose Jr (1796–1865) was a cousin of Daniel O'Connell and served as his land agent from 1822. In 1830 he married Ricarda Connor (1796–1848), daughter of Mary's sister, Betsey O'Connell (d. 1815), and Daniel O'Connell's law partner, James Connor (d. 1819). The missing Phil Primrose was John's brother. The *Kerry Evening Post* reported the accident on 2 November 1831 in which Charles Eagar, son of the Cahirciveen postmaster, also drowned. Apparently a funeral service was held after the search for the body ended. Another ceremony took place after the body was washed ashore.

19 The O'Connell family often used the term 'foster' when referring to the practice of sending their children out to be wet-nursed. All the O'Connell children appear to have been wet-nursed. Although Maurice and Morgan were sent out to nurses when the family was living in Kerry, it would appear that after the purchase of the first family home in Dublin a nurse was brought into the home. Generally these nurses came from Kerry and were frequently nursing children of their own. From the family correspondence it would appear that each child maintained a special relationship with their 'foster family' throughout their lives. Mary's pointed reference in this collection of letters to the fact that Julia O'Brien and Ricarda Primrose were nursing their infants themselves, suggests that maternal breastfeeding was only a recent trend. See Erin I. Bishop, 'The World of Mary O'Connell, 1778–1836' (Ph.D. thesis, University College, Dublin, 1996).

20   A leading competitor of O'Connell's Brewery, Sweetman's Brewery was founded by the United Irishman John Sweetman (1752–1826). Operating as early as 1780, the company was one of the few to survive well into the late nineteenth century. See Patrick Lynch and John Vaizey, *Guinness's Brewery in the Irish Economy, 1759–1876* (Cambridge, 1960), pp. 93, 199.

21   Mary misdated this letter. The date 25 November fell on a Friday. The correct date is Saturday, 26 November 1831.

22   Perhaps Mary refers to O'Connell's speech before the National Political Union on 6 December in which he accused Bishop Doyle of bestowing undue praise upon the Anglesey administration which O'Connell claimed had done nothing for the people.

23   Valentine Browne Lawless (1773–1853), 2nd Baron Cloncurry's scathing attack on O'Connell appeared in *The Pilot* on 11 January 1832. In it Cloncurry outlined the reasons why he would not attend the proposed assembly of Irish members of parliament in Dublin: he believed that the meeting would only 'aid Mr O'Connell in either forcing him into office, or of drawing from our poor and generous People a farther portion of the wretched pittance remaining to them,' and that the assembly would only serve 'to register the decrees of Mr O'Connell, most of which have latterly had their origin in selfishness, in disordered excitement, or in bad passion'. He further accused O'Connell of regularly stating as fact 'what he knows no rational being could believe'. James Warren Doyle (1786–1834), the Catholic Bishop of Kildare and Leighlin, issued another attack against O'Connell in the same issue of the *The Pilot*. Doyle accused O'Connell of too frequently changing his opinion, which, in turn, undermined his authority. He demanded an explanation of how O'Connell could 'combat the establishment of a legal provision for the Irish Poor'. He further accused O'Connell of misrepresenting to the public the plan of relief. See *DNB* entries for Lawless and Doyle.

24   When the Prince Regent became King George IV in 1820, Ernest Augustus, Duke of Cumberland (1771–1851), the fifth son of George III, gained substantial power. The death of Princess Charlotte and the Duke of York brought him even nearer to the throne. William IV's accession in 1830, however, greatly diminished Cumberland's influence in politics. William IV married Adelaide, the eldest daughter of George, Duke of Saxe-Coburg-Meiningen, in 1818. The couple had two daughters, both of whom died in infancy. Cumberland's opposition to the Reform Bill of 1832 and his position as Grand Master of the Irish Orangemen made him a political enemy of the O'Connells. See *DNB* entries for Ernest Augustus, Duke of Cumberland, and William IV.

Bibliography

Manuscripts

O'Connell Correspondence (National Library of Ireland)
    MS 13644 (4) [10, 21]
    MS 13644 (5) [6]
    MS 13644 (9) [5, 7, 8, 12, 16, 18–20, 22–26, 28–30, 32–34, 38, 39, 41]
    MS 13644 (10) [43–53]
    MS 13644 (11) [9, 11, 13, 14, 17, 27, 35–37, 40, 42]
    MS 13645 (6) [31]
    MS 13645 (7) [15]
O'Connell–Fitz-Simon Papers. Microfilm (National Library of Ireland)
    Microfilm P. 1621–2 [1–4]

Published Documents and Letters

Battersby W. J. (ed.), *A Complete Catholic Directory, Almanack and Registry* (Dublin, 1836) *Hansard's Parliamentary Debates*.

O'Connell, M. R. (ed.). *The Correspondence of Daniel O'Connell* (8 vols, Shannon, 1972–80)

Secondary Sources

Bartlett, Thomas, *The Fall and Rise of the Irish Nation: The Catholic Question, 1690–1830* (Dublin, 1992)

Bishop, Erin I., 'The World of Mary O'Connell, 1778–1836' (Ph.D. thesis, University College, Dublin, 1996)

Boyce, D. George, *Nineteenth-Century Ireland: The Search for Stability* (Dublin, 1990)

Clarkson, L. A., 'Love, Labour and Life: Women in Carrick-on-Suir in the Late Eighteenth Century', *Irish Economic and Social History*, xx (1993), pp. 18–24

Connolly, S. J., 'The "Blessed Turf": Cholera and Popular Panic in Ireland, June 1832', *Irish Historical Studies*, xxiii (1982–83), pp. 214–32

Cott, Nancy F., *The Bonds of Womanhood: 'Woman's Sphere' in New England, 1780–1835* (New Haven, 1977)

Craig, Maurice, *Dublin, 1660–1860* (Dublin, 1969)

Daly, Mary E., *Social and Economic History of Ireland since 1800* (Dublin, 1981)

Davidoff, Lenore, and Hall, Catherine, *Family Fortunes: Men and Women of the English Middle Class, 1780–1850* (London, 1992)

Durey, Michael, *The Return of the Plague: British Society and the Cholera, 1831–32* (Dublin, 1979)

Edwards, R. Dudley, *Daniel O'Connell and his World* (London, 1975)

Lewis, Judith, *In the Family Way: Childbearing in the British Aristocracy, 1750–1860* (New Brunswick, 1986)

Lynch, Patrick, and Vaizey John, *Guinness's Brewery in the Irish Economy, 1759–1876* (Cambridge, 1960)

McCartney, Donal, *The Dawning of Democracy: Ireland 1800–1870* (Dublin, 1987)

—— (ed.), *The World of Daniel O'Connell* (Dublin, 1980)

MacDonagh, Oliver, *O'Connell: The Life of Daniel O'Connell, 1775–1847* (London, 1991)

Morris, R. J., *Cholera 1832: The Social Response to an Epidemic* (New York, 1976)

O'Connell, M. R., *Daniel O'Connell: The Man and his Politics* (Dublin, 1990)

O'Ferrall, Fergus, *Daniel O'Connell* (Dublin, 1981)

—— *Catholic Emancipation: Daniel O'Connell and the Birth of Irish Democracy, 1820–1830* (Dublin, 1985)

Ó Tuathaigh, Gearóid, *Ireland before the Famine, 1798–1848* (Dublin, 1990)

Stone, Lawrence, *The Family, Sex and Marriage in England, 1500–1800* (London, 1977)

Trumbach, Randolph, *The Rise of the Egalitarian Family* (New York, 1978)

Index